MANAGING EDITOR
Natalie Earnheart

CREATIVE DIRECTOR
Christine Ricks

PHOTOGRAPHER
BPD Studios

CONTRIBUTING PHOTOGRAPHERS
Heidi Stock, Lauren Dorton

VIDEOGRAPHER
Jake Doan

TECHNICAL WRITER
Edie McGinnis

TECHNICAL EDITOR
Jane Miller, Denise Lane

PATTERN LAYOUT DESIGN
Ally Simmons

PROJECT DESIGN TEAM
Natalie Earnheart, Jenny Doan,
Sarah Galbraith

AUTHOR OF THE FAIR THIEF
Steve Westover

CONTRIBUTING COPY WRITERS
Jenny Doan, Natalie Earnheart, Christine
Ricks, Katie Mifsud, Camille Maddox,
Nichole Spravzoff, Edie McGinnis

COPY EDITOR
Nichole Spravzoff

CONTRIBUTING PIECERS
Jenny Doan, Natalie Earnheart,
Carol Henderson, Cindy Morris, Sherry
Whitt, Janice Richardson

CONTRIBUTING QUILTERS
Jamey Stone-Quilting Department Manager,
Debbie Allen-Daytime Assistant Manager,
Sarah Richardson, Angela Wilson, Tory
Wood, Linda Frump, Debbie Elder, Betty
Bates, Lynette Powers, Rachel Hale, Karla
Zinkand, Deloris Burnett, Bernice Kelly,
Kara Snow, Devin Ragle, Janet Caselman,
Nikki LaPiana, Michaela Butterfield, Rachael
Joyce, Bruce Van Iperen, Seth Wynne

PRINTING COORDINATOR
Rob Stoebener

PRINTING SERVICES
Walsworth Print Group
803 South Missouri
Marceline, MO 64658

CONTACT US
Missouri Star Quilt Company
114 N Davis
Hamilton, Mo. 64644
888-571-1122
info@missouriquiltco.com

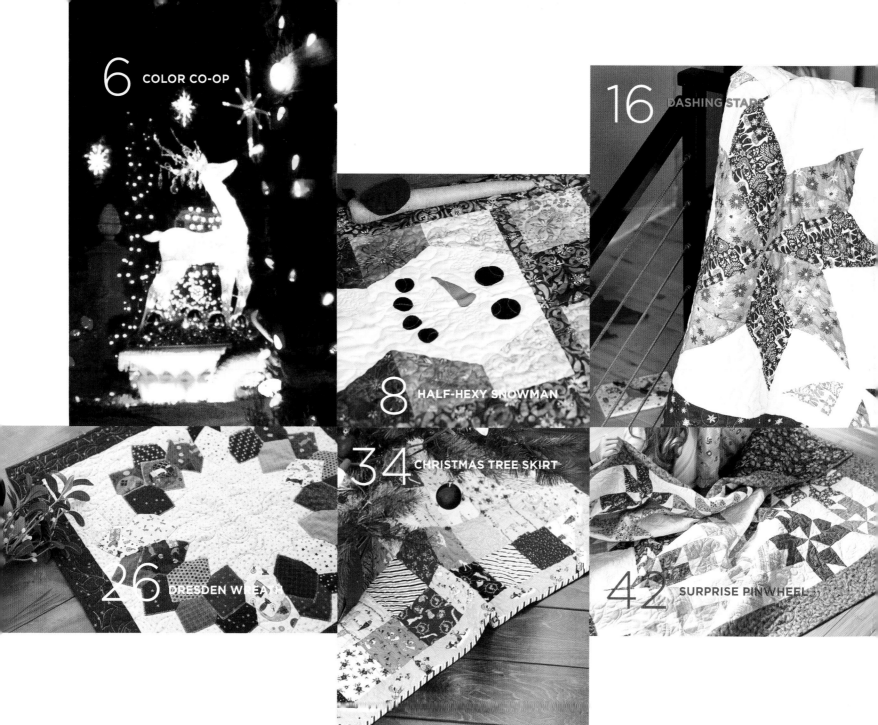

content

Ooops! Sometimes we make mistakes.
To find corrections to every issue of Block
go to: **www.msqc.co/corrections**

hello
from MSQC

I have the privilege of traveling all over the world and I honestly believe that I get to meet the best people ever! You quilters are such an inspiration to me. You're so kind and giving. As I write this letter to you, I am sitting on a balcony, looking out into the turquoise ocean. The palm trees are gently swaying in the breeze and the air is warm and floral. I am miles away from my home in rural Missouri. In all my life I honestly never thought I'd be in a place like this. What a marvelous opportunity to teach in such beautiful places throughout the world. Last week I was in Canada and I felt so warmly welcomed in the cold North. Wonderful people are all over this big world and if you're ever feeling kind of small, wondering what difference you make, I want to tell you that you do make a difference. Whether our circle is large or small, we all have the power to help people every day.

Summertime fills me with warmth and brings my heart joy. It's a time to slow down and let ourselves soak up with sunshine. And I've got to save up plenty for the long, cold Midwest winter! These warm summer memories keep me going throughout the indoor quilting season, which isn't too far away, but I don't mind when the temperature drops because that means the holidays are coming! I like to get a little head start on my Christmas list, so this issue of Block is filled with fun gift ideas for all your loved ones and fall projects to decorate your home. For now, I'll be thinking of all of you, sending you plenty of Aloha from the island of Kauai. Enjoy the fleeting days of summer and try to squeeze in one last little getaway. You deserve it!

JENNY DOAN
MISSOURI STAR QUILT CO

CHRISTMAS
is coming ...

When it's 100 degrees outside it's hard for me to think that Christmas is just around the corner. Because of the nature of my job producing a holiday magazine in the middle of July, I'm forced to embrace the fact that Christmas is coming. The upside is that it helps me start thinking about the many handmade gifts I want to make for family and friends.

As I sit by the lake still reveling in the warmer days my mind wanders to cooler temperatures and heart warming gifts that will be recieved with love and joy. Enjoy what's left of your summer—but start thinking about those holiday projects now so you won't be left to the last minute trying to pull things together. Here's some holiday inspiration to get those ideas churning. Happy making!

CHRISTINE RICKS
MSQC Creative Director, BLOCK MAGAZINE

SOLIDS

FBY1537   Bella Solids Natural
by Moda Fabrics for Moda Fabrics
SKU: 9900 12

FBY1281   Bella Solids Aqua
by Moda Fabrics for Moda Fabrics
SKU: 9900 34

FBY1277   Bella Solids Royal
by Moda Fabrics for Moda Fabrics
SKU: 9900 19

FBY42745   Bella Solids - Parfait Pink
by Moda Fabrics for Moda Fabrics
SKU: 9900 248

FBY12154   Bella Solids - Popsicle
by Moda Fabrics
SKU: 9900 143

FBY1771   Bella Solids - Dill
by Moda Fabrics for Moda Fabrics
SKU: 9900 77

PRINTS

FBY37963   Scandi 3 - Trees Linen
by The Henley Studio for Makower UK
SKU: 1592-Q

FBY37450   The Cookie Exchange - Joy Splash
by Sweetwater for Moda Fabrics
SKU: 5624 16

FBY39032   Garland - Ornamentals Teal
by Cotton + Steel for Cotton+Steel
SKU: 5073-2

FBY41036   Cozy Christmas - Cozy Stripe Pink
by Lori Holt for Riley Blake
SKU: C5368-PINK

FBY38043   Pixie Noel - Pixie Hats and Socks Red
by Tasha Noel for Riley Blake
SKU: C5253-RED

FBY38117   Backyard Roses - Backyard Bouquet Green
by Nadra Ridgeway of Ellis & Higgs for Riley Blake
SKU: C5291-GREEN

half-hexy snowman *table runner*

quilt designed by *Missouri Star Quilt Company*

One of the things I love about living in the country is how much time we spend outdoors. Whatever the time of year, my kids could always be found exploring, fishing, building, and having a blast outside. I love to repeat the old saying: "There is no such thing as bad weather, only inappropriate clothing," so for me, winter is no excuse to stay inside.

The kids and I love making snowmen, and you know me, I can't make just a standard snowman. We've sculpted snow women, children, pets, and even aliens! So I thought nothing of it one wintry Saturday when the kids had spent hours in the yard making a whole host of snow people. A little after lunchtime one of the boys came in shouting, "Mom, Dad! You've got to see what we made. You're not gonna believe it!" Ron and I bundled up and headed outside, ready to be amazed by how many snowmen they'd made. We gazed across the lawn and saw that there must

For the tutorial and everything need you to make this quilt visit:
www.msqc.co/blockholiday16

have been a dozen. It was incredible! As we trudged out to the middle of the yard, admiring each snowman's unique look, suddenly the kids descended upon us from behind their snowmen where they were hiding piles of snowballs! Ron and I didn't waste a second, right away we were engaged in a snowball fight like you've never seen!

We dodged left and right, avoiding the icy blasts, and somehow we managed to scrape up a few large snowballs to retaliate! Ron's a pretty quick snowball maker, one of his admirable traits, and he'd quickly hand them off to me. I had a lazer-sharp aim and any child caught in my sights was covered in snow before he knew what had happened! The game continued on for a while until we ran out of breath and sagged to the ground, laughing, and covered in snow. Unfortunately, some of the snow people had suffered casualties. The ground was littered with fallen carrot noses and charcoal briquette eyes. I think they got the worst of it!

When we tell that story today, Ron and I always playfully boast about our glorious victory over those sneaky kids, but I have a feeling they might remember it a little differently.

" There is no such thing as bad weather, only inappropriate clothing. "

materials

makes a 19¼" X 45" table runner

TABLE RUNNER TOP
- (4) 10" white solid squares
- (4) 10" assorted dark print squares
- (2) 5" matching light print squares
- (1) 10" dark solid square for buttons, mouths and eyes
- (1) 2" x 4" scrap of orange for noses

SASHING, OUTER BORDER, BINDING
- ¾ yard dark print

OTHER SUPPLIES
- 10" x 12" rectangle paper-backed fusible web
- M3QC 10" Half-Hexagon Template

BACKING
- 1½ yards

SAMPLE QUILT
- **Artisan Batiks Noel** by Lunn Studios for Robert Kaufman

1 cut

From the white solid squares, cut:

- 8 half-hexagons – fold each of the white 10" squares in half. Place the short end of the half-hexagon template on the raw edge of the fabric. Cut around the template as shown. Each square will yield **2 half-hexagons**. 1A

From the assorted dark print 10" squares, cut:

- 16 quarter-hexagons – From each square, cut 2 half-hexagons (follow the directions for cutting

1A

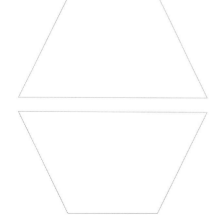

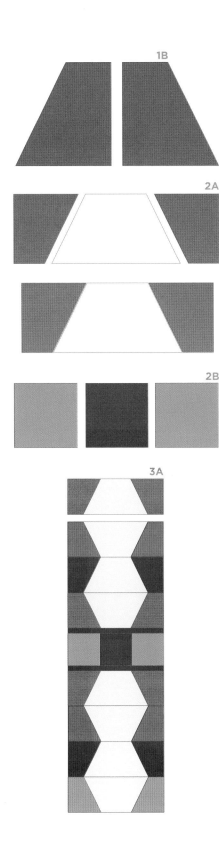

half-hexagons given for the white squares). Cut each half-hexagon in half to make **2 quarter-hexagons**. 1B

Cut a 10″ square of paper-backed fusible web. Trace 4 eyes and 12 mouth/button pieces, on page 15, onto the paper side. Press the fusible onto the reverse side of the dark solid 10″ square and cut out the shapes. Set them aside until you're ready to fuse them in place.

Trace 2 noses, on page 15, onto the remaining piece of fusible web. Press the fusible onto the reverse side of the orange rectangle. Cut out the shapes and set them aside until you're ready to fuse them in place.

From the dark print being used for the border and binding, cut:

- (1) 5″ square

- (1) 1½″ wide strip – subcut this strip into (2) 1½″ x 14¼″ rectangles.

Set the remaining fabric aside for the borders.

2 sew

Sew a dark print quarter-hexagon to either side of a white half-hexagon. Make **8 snowman units** and set aside for the moment. 2A

Sew a light 5″ square to either side of the dark print 5″ square you cut from the border fabric to make the center strip unit. 2B

3 lay out and sew

Lay out the snowman units, the center strip unit and the dark print rectangles as shown. 3A

Stitch the pieces together to complete the center. Position the appliqué pieces onto the snowmen as shown on page 15. Fuse in place and blanket stitch around each piece. 3B

4 borders

Cut (3) 3¼″ strips across the width of the fabric. Sew the strips together end-to-end to make one long strip. Trim the borders from this strip. Refer to Borders (pg. 108) in the Construction Basics to measure and cut the outer borders. The strips are approximately 40″ for the sides and approximately 19¾″ for the top and bottom.

5 quilt and bind

Layer the quilt with batting and backing and quilt. After the quilting is complete, square up the quilt and trim away all excess batting and backing. Add binding to complete the quilt. See Construction Basics (pg. 109) for binding instructions.

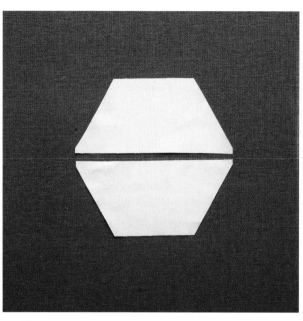

1 Using the MSQC 10″ Half-Hexagon Template, cut 8 shapes from the white squares.

2 Each square will yield 2 half-hexagons.

3 Cut 8 half-hexagon shapes from the assorted dark print squares.

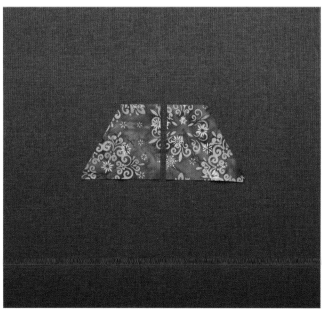

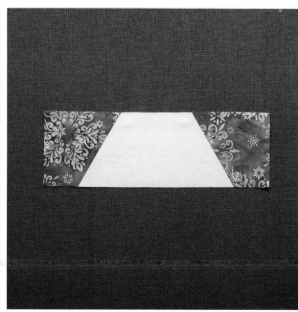

4 Cut the dark print half-hexagon shapes in half to make 16 quarter-hexagons

5 Sew a quarter-hexagon to either side of a white half-hexagon. Make 8.

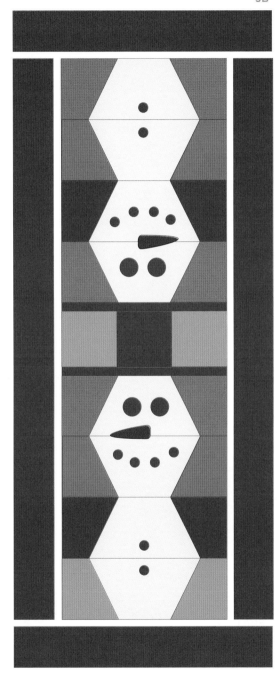

nose

mouth piece/
button

eye

For the tutorial and everything you need to make this quilt visit www.msqc.co/blockholiday16

dashing
stars

quilt designed by *Missouri Star Quilt Company*

My mother was the heart of our family. In those days, it was common for mothers to stay home and manage every detail of the home. Dad was great, but it was Mom who kept the place running! So when Mom contracted spinal meningitis, things kind of screeched to a halt.

Poor Dad did his best to race home from work each day, throw together something simple for dinner, and toss in a load of laundry before tucking us kids into bed, but it was hard on all of us. I was too young to understand how sick Mom really was, but I can still picture her, lying on the couch day after day.

As Christmas Eve drew near, Mom was still sick. Things weren't quite the same that holiday season. No fresh baked gingerbread cookies were waiting for us when we got home from school. We didn't go caroling with the neighbors. It was a subdued celebration, and it didn't feel quite right. Worst of all, for the first time in his life, Dad had to venture out all alone to do the Christmas shopping for my two siblings and me. Frankly, we were all a little nervous.

On Christmas morning there was a small package waiting for me under the tree. I had no idea what to expect! What on earth would Dad have chosen as my gift? I braced myself for the disappointment of new socks or underwear and began to tear gingerly at the wrapping.

Much to my surprise, it was a spy kit! Why Dad chose a spy kit, I'll never know, but I loved it! My whole life I had received very typically girly gifts: dolls, dress up clothes, play kitchen items, and the like, but I also had quite the tomboy streak, and this spy kit thrilled me to the core! It came with a badge,

glasses, a decoder ring, and a pen with disappearing ink. All during Christmas vacation I was busy creating codes and writing secret messages. I'm sure my mother was relieved to see me so happily occupied as our usual celebrations had been put on hold.

Time passed and Mom finally started to feel like herself again. Looking back, I'm sure that holiday season was overwhelmingly difficult for my parents, but thanks to my sweet dad, it is one of my most cherished memories.

materials

makes a 90" X 90" quilt

QUILT TOP
- 1 package of 10" squares (42 ct.) *plus* (3) 10" squares cut from outer border fabric
- 3 yards background fabric – includes sashing

INNER BORDER
- ¾ yard

OUTER BORDER
- 2 yards – includes fabric for cutting (3) 10" squares for blocks and (4) 2½" squares for cornerstones

BINDING
- ¾ yard

BACKING
- 8¼ yards - vertical seams

SAMPLE QUILT
- **Scandi 3** by The Henley Studio for Makower

1 cut

From the outer border fabric, cut:

- (1) 10" strip across the width of the fabric. Subcut the strip into (3) 10" squares and (4) 2½" squares. Add the squares to your package of 10" squares. Set the 2½" squares (cornerstones) aside until you are ready to sash the blocks together.

Set the remaining outer border fabric aside until you are ready to cut the borders.

From the package of 10" squares:

- Choose (9) 10" squares of assorted colors. Cut each into (4) 5" squares. Set aside for the moment.

From the background fabric, cut:

- (6) 6½" strips across the width of the fabric. Subcut the strips into 6½" squares for a total of 36 squares.

- (4) 10" strips across the width of the fabric. Subcut the strips into 10" squares for a total of 16 squares. You need (18) 10" squares but we will cut the remaining 2 in the next step.

- (1) 24½" strip across the width of the fabric. Subcut this strip VERTICALLY into (12) 2½" x 24½" sashing rectangles. Cut (2) 10" squares from the remaining fabric and put them in the stack of 10" background squares.

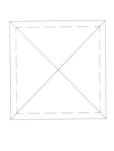
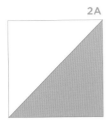

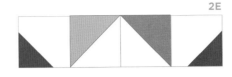

2A

2B

2E

2F

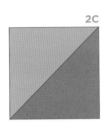

2C

2G

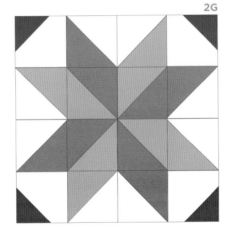

2D

facing. Sew around the perimeter using a ¼" seam allowance. Cut the stitched squares from corner to corner twice on the diagonal. Press open to reveal 4 matching light/background half-square triangle units. Square each to 6½". **2A**

Layer a dark print 10" square with a background 10" square with right sides facing. Sew around the perimeter using a ¼" seam allowance. Cut the stitched squares from corner to corner twice on the diagonal. Press open to reveal 4 matching dark/background half-square triangle units. Square each to 6½". **2B**

Layer a dark print 10" square with a light print 10" square with right sides facing. Sew around the perimeter using a ¼" seam allowance. Cut the stitched squares from corner to corner twice on the diagonal. Press open to reveal 4 matching dark/light half-square triangle units. Square each to 6½". **2C**

Press 4 matching 5" squares in half once on the diagonal with wrong sides facing to mark your sewing line. Open and place a square on one corner of a background 6½" square. Sew on the marked line. Trim the excess fabric away ¼" from the stitched seam. We'll call these "corner units" for the sake of clarity. **2D**

2 block construction

Select 2 matching light squares and 2 matching dark squares from the package of 10" squares. If you don't have matching squares, don't fret. Just chose squares that are the same color rather than the same print. They will blend together perfectly!

Layer a light print 10" square with a background 10" square with right sides

Sew a corner unit to a light/background half-square triangle unit. Add a dark/background half-square triangle unit then another corner unit. **Make 2 rows** like this. **2E**

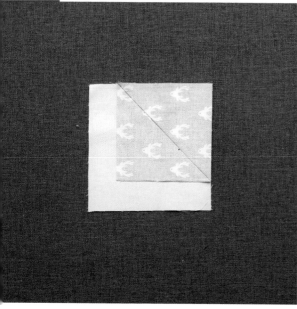

1   Place a marked 5″ square on the corner of a 6 ½″ background square and sew on the line.

2   Trim the excess fabric ¼″ away from the sewn seam.

3   After the unit has been trimmed, open and press the seam allowance toward the darker fabric.

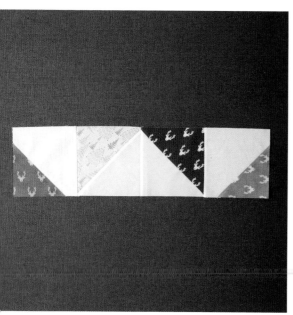

4   Sew a corner unit to a light/background half-square triangle unit. Add a dark/background half-square triangle unit then another corner unit. Make two rows like this.

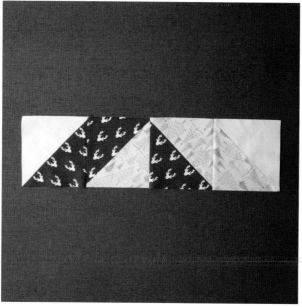

5   Sew a dark/background half-square triangle unit to a dark/light half-square triangle. Add another dark/light half-square triangle unit then a light/background half-square triangle. Make 2 rows like this.

6   Sew the 4 rows together to complete the block.

Sew a dark/background half-square triangle unit to a dark/light half-square triangle unit. Add another dark/light half-square triangle unit then a light/background half-square triangle unit. **Make 2** rows like this. 2F

Sew the 4 rows together to complete the block. **Make 9 blocks.** 2G

3 lay out blocks and sashing

Lay out the blocks in **3 rows** with each row having **3 blocks.** When you are happy with the arrangement, sew the rows together, adding a sashing rectangle between each block.

Make a sashing strip by sewing a sashing rectangle to a 2½" print square that you cut from the border fabric earlier. Add another sashing rectangle and another print 2½" square. End the strip with a sashing rectangle. **Make 2** and sew them between each row. 3A

3A

4 inner border

Cut (8) 2½" strips across the width of the fabric. Sew the strips together end-to-end to make one long strip. Trim the borders from this strip.

Refer to Borders (pg. 108) in the Construction Basics to measure and cut the inner borders. The strips are approximately 80½" for the sides and approximately 90½" for the top and bottom.

5 outer border

Cut (9) 5½" strips across the width of the fabric. Sew the strips together end-to-end to make one long strip. Trim the borders from this strip.

Refer to Borders (pg. 108) in the Construction Basics to measure and cut the outer borders. The strips are approximately 80½" for the sides and approximately 90½" for the top and bottom.

6 quilt and bind

Layer the quilt with batting and backing and quilt. After the quilting is complete, square up the quilt and trim away all excess batting and backing. Add binding to complete the quilt. See Construction Basics (pg. 109) for binding instructions.

dresden
wreath

quilt designed by *Missouri Star Quilt Company*

The kids and I are not known for our quiet and timid ways. On the contrary, we're loud and happy and a whole lot of fun, if I do say so myself! We enjoy big crowds and lively celebrations, and we LOVE to sing. So you can bet that when Christmastime rolls around, we're ready to party our hearts out with a good old fashioned round of caroling!

Every year we set out for a night of caroling in Hamilton with the whole family in tow. My daughter Sarah puts together platters of Christmas cookies to take to all the businesses in town. We wrap up in our warmest coats and mittens, and even the littlest Doans join in as we carol our way down Main Street.

Hamilton is a small town with only a handful of businesses, so we're able to hit them all in one evening, from the antiques shop to the florist, and yes, even the local bar. Oh, the bar. As long as I live, I'll always remember the first time we caroled at the bar.

I had never in my life been inside a bar—we're more of a cookies and punch kind of family. Not knowing what to expect, we burst through the doors into the poorly lit entrance and stood there for what seemed like forever, just

For the tutorial and everything you need to make this quilt visit: www.msqc.co/blockholiday16

silently blinking, trying to adjust to the dim light.I could feel several sets of surprised eyes on me, watching in disbelief as we marched to the center of the room and began singing with gusto:

"We wish you a Merry Christmas! We wish you a Merry Christmas! We wish you a Merry Christmas, and a Happy New Year!"

When we finished, with the echo of our voices still in the air, we were greeted with silence—thick, lingering silence.

And then, an older man sitting at the table next to us said, "Well, they sure are nice singers."

We quickly handed him the plate of cookies and hightailed it our of there, smiling all the way.

I heard later from the owner of the bar that we were the first carolers they'd ever had, and, well, that made me glad, because I've yet to find a person or place that isn't made better by a little touch of the Christmas spirit!

So on lives our caroling tradition, but now folks have come to expect our visits. And if you plan to open up shop in Hamilton, be prepared for your own private concert from the caroling Doans!

" I've yet to find a person or place that isn't made better by a little touch of the Christmas spirit! "

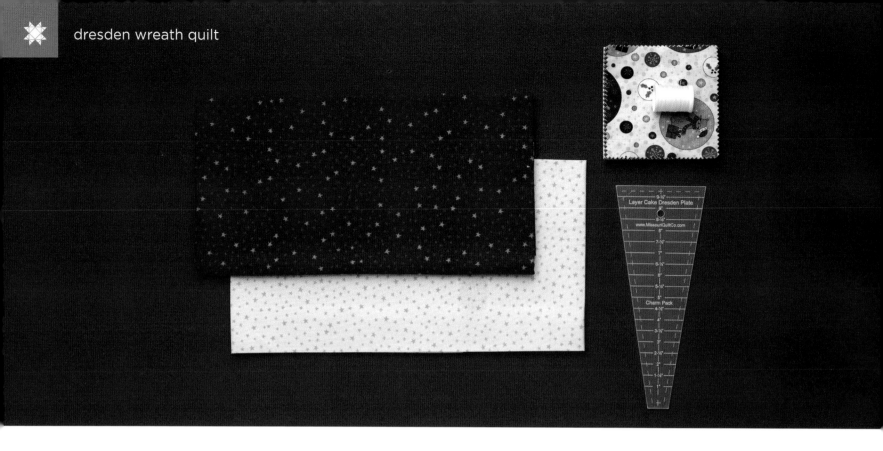

materials

makes a 28" X 28" quilt

QUILT TOP
- 1 package 5" squares
- ¾ yard background fabric

BORDER
- ½ yard

BINDING
- ½ yard

BACKING
- 1 yard

ADDITIONAL SUPPLIES
- MSQC Dresden Template

SAMPLE QUILT
- **Festive Fun** by Lynette Anderson Designs for RJR

1 cut

From the 5" print squares, cut:

- 36 blades using the MSQC Dresden Plate template. Align the **widest** part of the template with the top of the squares when cutting.

From the background fabric, cut:

- (1) 24½" square

2 sew

Select 20 blades for the outer wreath. Fold each in half vertically and stitch across the end. Open and press. **2A 2B**

2A

2B

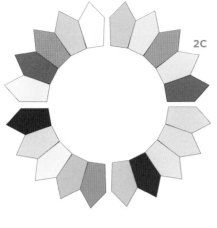

2C

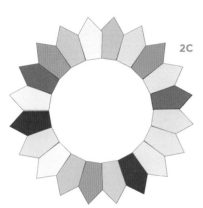

2C

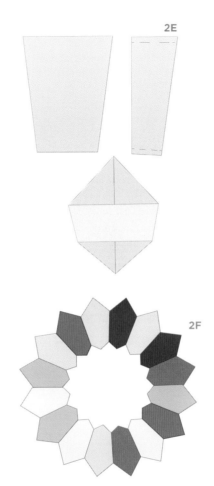

2E

2F

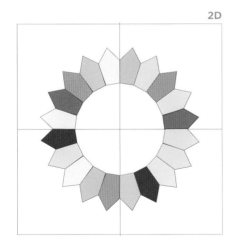

2D

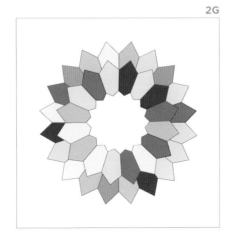

2G

Begin at the top of a blade and sew it to the next. Join 5 blades. Set aside. Join 5 more, repeat until you have made **4 sections** of **5 blades each**. Join the 4 sections together to make 1 large circle. You can also sew them all together into one large circle if you'd rather. Breaking them into the 4 groups just makes the wreath easier to handle. **2C**

Fold the background fabric in half horizontally and vertically. Lightly crease the folds for placement purposes. Pin the wreath to the background fabric, aligning the seams of the 4 sections with the fold marks. **2D**

Appliqué the outer edge of the wreath to the background fabric using a small buttonhole stitch.

Sew across BOTH ends of the **remaining 16 blades**. Open and press. **2E**

Sew the blades together into sections as before. This time you will have **4 blades** per section. Sew the sections together to make a circle. **2F**

Place the smaller wreath on top of the larger wreath and pin in place. Because this wreath has fewer blades, it should rest closer to the center of the piece. As you pin, make certain it lies flat before you begin sewing. Don't hesitate to take a few seams in a bit if it's not flat. **2G**

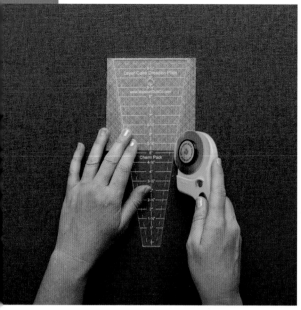

1 Align the top of the MSQC Dresden Plate Template with the top of a 5″ square. Cut the shape.

2 Sew across the top of each of 20 blades.

3 Open the blade and press the piece flat.

4 When making the inner wreath pieces, sew across both ends of each blade.

5 Open the piece and press the points flat.

6 Layer the outer and inner rings of the wreath onto the background fabric. Stitch in place using a blanket stitch.

Appliqué the smaller wreath in place using a buttonhole stitch on the outside and the inside edge. Press.

3 border

Cut (3) 2½" strips across the width of the fabric. Sew the strips together end-to-end to make one long strip. Trim the borders from this strip.

Refer to Borders (pg. 108) in the Construction Basics to measure and cut the outer borders. The strips are approximately 24½" for the sides and approximately 28½" for the top and bottom.

4 quilt and bind

Layer the quilt with batting and backing and quilt. After the quilting is complete, square up the quilt and trim away all excess batting and backing. Add binding to complete the quilt. See Construction Basics (pg. 109) for binding instructions.

For the tutorial and everything
you need to make this quilt visit:
www.msqc.co/blockholiday16

christmas
tree skirt

quilt designed by *Missouri Star Quilt Company*

I wish I could always see Christmas through the eyes of children. To them everything seems so magical. I love spending the holidays surrounded by my sweet grandchildren. They are special little people and bring me so much joy! They are often featured in this very magazine and we have a lot of fun behind the scenes. A while back, my grandson, Ezra, accompanied us on a photoshoot featuring a Christmas Tree Skirt. The shot was supposed to have three children sitting under the tree, surrounded by presents. So my daughter in law, Misty, got her children ready and a couple of us got busy and wrapped some empty boxes so that they would look like presents. We placed the presents all around the children and they seemed as full of excitement as they would have been on Christmas day!

After the photoshoot was over, Ezra looked up at me and asked if he could open the presents. Not thinking too much about it, I said yes. He energetically tore the paper off the box and took a long, silent look inside. Then, with all the enthusiasm he could muster, he yelled at the top of his

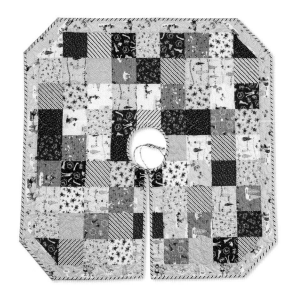

lungs, "An iron! I got an iron!" He then opened the box and upon looking inside, found it empty except for the directions, but that didn't deter him. He then yelled, "Directions! I got directions!" We laughed and laughed until our sides hurt. I love the simplicity of children.

Ezra's innocent reaction to his "gift" reminds me of a simpler time in our family when we didn't have much extra money for fancy store-bought gifts. We wanted to teach our children to be grateful for what they had and it wasn't always easy, but small acts of kindness make all the difference. Giving helps us see that there are always others who need our help and in turn, we feel more grateful for what we have been given.

At our church there was a Christmas tree that had names on it instead of ornaments. Each paper slip held the name of a child in need, their age, their gender, and an item that they might enjoy. One read "a clock radio," another "a pair of shoes, size 4," and yet another, "a Barbie doll." Each piece of paper was a Christmas wish waiting to be fulfilled. When my children spied that beautifully decorated tree, they immediately flocked to it. Then their faces became more serious as they started reading the slips of paper. I asked them if they wanted to help make some of these wishes come true and they emphatically agreed.

We went home that night and they retreated to their rooms, seeking out the items written on the papers. Each came back with something they had polished up and were ready to give to someone else. I could tell it was a genuine sacrifice for them, but they smiled as we wrapped them up to place under that tree.

They realized that year that Christmas wasn't so much about what presents they would or would not be getting—although I received plenty of Christmas lists, handwritten in crayon. It became a more meaningful experience as they reached out to help others.

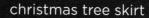

materials

makes a 45" x 45" tree skirt

TREE SKIRT TOP
• 2 packages of 5″ print squares

BORDER
• ¾ yard

BINDING AND TIES
• ¾ yard

BACKING
• 3 yards - vertical seam(s)

Optional   freezer paper

SAMPLE QUILT
• **Pixie Noel** by Tasha Noel for Riley Blake

1 lay out the top

Lay out the squares in rows. You need **9 squares** across in each row and you need **9 rows.** Sew the rows together when you are happy with your arrangement.

Press the odd numbered rows toward the right and the even numbered rows toward the left. That will make the seams nest together. **1A**

2 border

From the border fabric, cut (7) 2¾″ strips across the width of the fabric. Sew the strips together end-to-end to make

1A

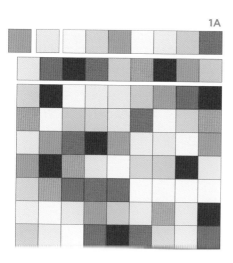

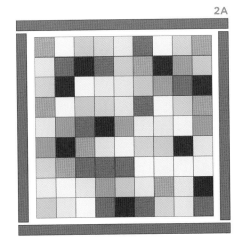

2A

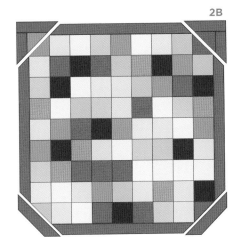

2B

one long strip. Trim the borders from this strip.

Refer to Borders (pg. 108) in the Construction Basics to measure and cut the borders. The strips are approximately 41″ for the sides and approximately 45½″ for the top and bottom. You will also need to cut (4) 15″ strips for the corner borders.

Sew the side borders in place then add the top and bottom borders. 2A

In one corner, mark a diagonal line that crosses over the outer square at a 45-degree angle. Trim the corner ¼″ away from the marked line. Refer to the corner diagram and repeat for all 4 corners.

Sew a border strip to the corner of the quilt. Trim the strip evenly with the edge of the quilt on both sides. Repeat for the remaining corners. 2B

3 finishing

Layer the quilt with batting and backing and quilt.

Find the center of the tree skirt by folding it in half lengthwise, then vertically. Mark the center with a pin or a marking pen.

Trace a 4½″ circle using the template provided onto a piece of freezer paper. Cut out the freezer paper circle and press the shiny side of the paper to the center of the tree skirt. On one side of the skirt, draw a line from the circle to the outer edge. Cut along the line and around the circle. 3A

4 binding and ties

Add binding to the unfinished edges of the tree skirt, including the split and the circle. See pg. 109 in the general directions for binding instructions.

From the binding fabric, cut (2) 1¼″ x 12″ rectangles. Press under ¼″ along the long sides of each rectangle and on one end. Fold the rectangles in half with wrong sides facing. Topstitch close to the pressed edges to finish the tie. 4A

Sew a tie to either side of the circle to complete your tree skirt. 4B

1 Layout 5″ squares in rows. Each row will be made up of 9 squares and you need 9 rows.

2 Add the border strips to the outer edges of the quilt.

3 Trim each corner at a 45-degree angle.

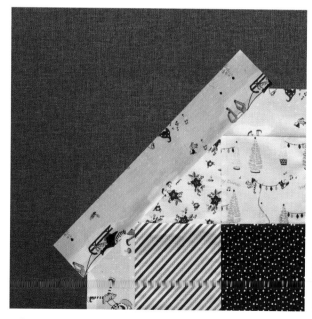

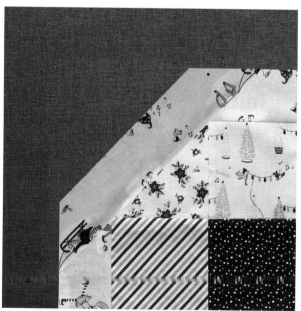

4 Add a short border strip to each corner.

5 Trim the ends of the corner border strips evenly with the edges of the quilt.

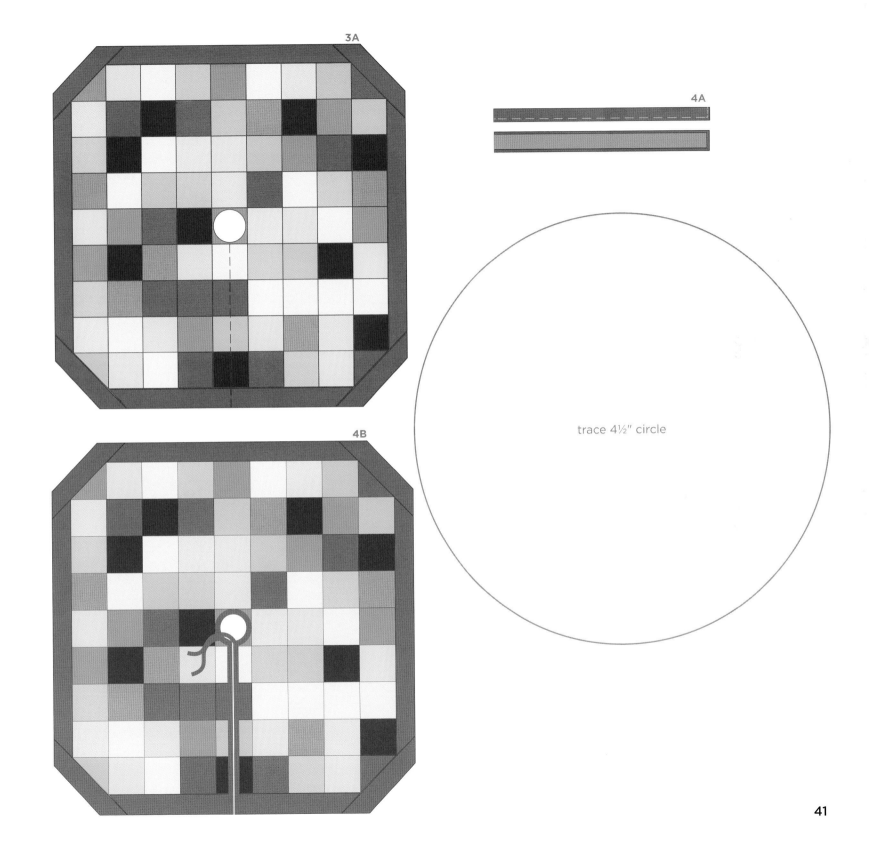

3A

4A

4B

trace 4½" circle

41

For the tutorial and everything
you need to make this quilt visit:
www.msqc.co/blockholiday16

surprise pinwheel

quilt designed by *Missouri Star Quilt Company*

My husband Ron shared one of his favorite Christmas memories with me. At times we may all lose that sense of Christmas wonder, but it only takes a little effort to bring the holiday spirit back into our homes. This is what Ron's parents did for him as a child. Here's the story in his words:

"There comes a time during childhood when we all begin to question the existence of Santa Claus. You want to believe, but it just seems so impossible and doubts inevitably start to creep in. Kids at school talk about spying presents in closets and parents eating cookies left out on Christmas Eve, and just the whole idea of a magical man who flies through the sky with a team of reindeer doesn't quite add up.

"When I was about seven years old, I started to have serious doubts about Old St. Nick. Consequently, as the holidays drew nearer, I found myself missing that little spark of excitement that accompanies the Christmas season. I think my parents noticed that I needed a little boost, because they really made that Christmas special for me and my sister.

43

"A few nights before Christmas, Dad called the family together to go for a ride in our '59 Chevy Impala. Dad, Mom, my sister Debbie, and I all piled in the car and headed out to look at Christmas lights. After about half an hour, Dad said he had forgotten something and took us back home. He ran in for just a minute and we were off again. There were several neighborhoods around us that really went all out on their Christmas decorations. We spent hours enjoying the lights displays and nativities. I still remember how peaceful it felt to sit in the warm car in the dark while Dad drove us past all those beautifully decorated homes wrapped in glowing lights.

Ron and his sister Debbie with Santa Claus

"After what felt like hours, we made our way back home. I felt so comfortable and drowsy after our long drive, but when I opened the front door, I was shocked wide awake. The whole living room looked like a scene out of the Sears Wish Book! There were decorations everywhere and presents piled high under the tree! Who could have possibly done it? Santa must have come while we were gone. In that moment I was sure Santa was real and he even knew where I lived."

materials

makes a 65" X 87" quilt

QUILT TOP
- 1 roll 2½" strips
- 3 yards background fabric

BORDER
- 1¼ yards

BINDING
- ¾ yard

BACKING
- 5¼ yards - vertical seam(s)

SAMPLE QUILT
- **Juniper Berry** by BasicGrey for Moda

1 cut

From each of 35 of the 2½" strips, cut:

- (4) 6" rectangles
- (4) 4" rectangles

Stack all rectangles cut from the same strip together.

From the background fabric, cut:

- (14) 4" strips across the width of the fabric - subcut the strips into 4" squares for a **total of 140.**
- (18) 2½" strips across the width of the fabric - subcut the strips into 2½" squares for a **total of 280.**

2 make a block

Fold and press a crease on the diagonal in each of (8) 2½" background squares. The crease will be your sewing line. 2A

Select a stack of 4" and 6" rectangles that use the same fabric. Stitch a 2½" square onto the end of the 6" rectangle.

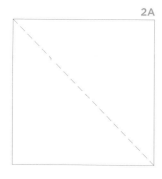

2A

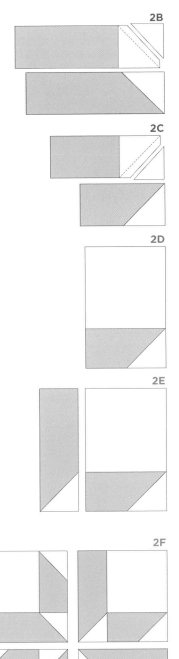

Notice the direction the square is sewn in place. Trim the excess fabric ¼" away from the sewn seam. All 6" rectangles have the square sewn on the same end and at the same angle. **2B**

Stitch a background 2½" square to the end of a 4" rectangle. Notice that this rectangle is a mirror image of the 6" rectangle. All 4" rectangles have the square sewn on the same end and at the same angle. **2C**

Stitch a 4" rectangle to a 4" background square. **Make 4. 2D**

Add a 6" rectangle to the left side as shown. This makes up one quadrant of the block. **Make 4. 2E**

Sew the 4 quadrants together to complete the block. **Make 35. 2F**

Block Size: 11" x 11" finished

3 lay out blocks

Arrange your blocks in rows with each row containing **5 blocks. Make 7 rows.**

Sew the rows together.

4 border

Cut (8) 5½" strips across the width of the fabric. Sew the strips together end-to-end to make one long strip. Trim the borders from this strip.

Refer to Borders (pg. 108) in the Construction Basics to measure and cut the outer borders. The strips are approximately 77½" for the sides and approximately 65½" for the top and bottom.

5 quilt and bind

Layer the quilt with batting and backing and quilt. After the quilting is complete, square up the quilt and trim away all excess batting and backing. Add binding to complete the quilt. See Construction Basics (pg. 109) for binding instructions.

1 Place a creased 2½″ square on the end of a 2½″ x 6″ strip with right sides facing. Sew on the creased line, then trim ¼″ away from the sewn seam.

2 Place a creased 2½″ square on the end of a 2½″ x 4″ strip with right sides facing. Sew on the creased line, then trim ¼″ away from the sewn seam. Notice that this seam is at a different angle than used on the 6″ strip.

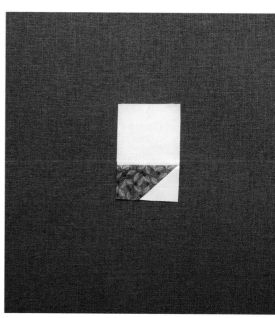

3 Sew the snowballed 4″ rectangle to a 4″ square.

4 Add a snowballed 6″ rectangle to the adjacent side of the square. Make 4.

5 Sew the 4 quadrants together to complete the block.

For the tutorial and everything
you need to make this quilt visit:
www.msqc.co/blockholiday16

courthouse steps

quilt designed by *Missouri Star Quilt Company*

In our family we adore surprises. The anticipation and planning always makes life a little more exciting! Around the holidays we always choose names for Secret Santa. When the children were younger they would try their very best not to blab the name of the person they chose and then go about doing one kind deed each day for that person for an entire week. It could be anything from making their bed and leaving a little treat on their pillow to cleaning the toilet for them before they could get to it. Somehow they forgot they were actually just doing each others' chores and it became a joy instead of a burden.

When the children got a little older, we started to think about the people outside of our family and how we might make their holidays brighter. One year a thought struck me as I was humming "The 12 Days of Christmas" to myself. Why not come up with a string of gifts to give to someone who needed a little cheer and make the gifts related to the song? I giggled to myself with anticipation and rounded up the kids. When I explained my idea

51

to them, they were ecstatic! We planned each of our 12 Days of Christmas gifts and some were pretty clever. One child came up with the idea that for "five golden rings" we should give a box of Cheerios! Another had the idea that for "two turtledoves," the gift should be Dove chocolates and a bar of Dove soap. How fun! Each gift was simple, but heartfelt. But we still hadn't decided who to give the gifts to just yet.

My neighbor kept popping into my head as the right person for the gifts, so I told the children that we'd have to be extra sneaky and deliver them after she left for work—she worked the night shift—so we wouldn't get caught. They were excited for the chance to stay up a little later too. Each night, from the 13th to the 24th of December, one lucky child would scurry over to the porch, leave the gift and attached note, and scurry back. We never got caught. And I didn't think much more about the 12 Days of Christmas ... until that July.

I was out mowing my front lawn when my neighbor approached me suddenly and asked, "are you the 12 Days of Christmas?" I was so taken aback that I coughed a little and squeaked out a feeble "yes." A huge smile spread across her face and before I knew it, she had me in a firm embrace. She told me how much the small gifts had meant to her and how her mother had passed away earlier that December. It had made her holidays so much happier finding these little surprises on her doorstep.

I'll never forget that Christmas and the lessons it taught. Those wonderful traditions are now being carried on to the next generation. Last year I got to ride along with several of my children's families as they snuck up to their neighbors' homes, rang the bell, left a treat, and ran back to the car. Seeing the excitement on their faces brought me right back to those 12 magical nights so many years ago.

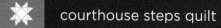

materials

makes a 76" X 76" quilt

QUILT TOP
- 1 roll of 2½" print strips
- 1 roll of 2½" background strips

NARROW INNER BORDERS
- ¾ yard background

outer border
- 1½" yards

BINDING
- ¾ yard

BACKING
- 4¾ yards - vertical seam(s)

SAMPLE QUILT
- **Holly Night Metallic** by Sentimental Studios for Moda

1 cut

 NOTE: *in order to make the most of your fabric, cut the longest strips first.*

From the background roll, cut:

- (16) 2½" x 14½" strips
- (32) 2½" x 10½" strips
- (32) 2½" x 6½" strips
- (24) 2½" squares

From the print roll, cut:

- (16) 2½" x 14½" strips
- (32) 2½" x 10½" strips
- (32) 2½" x 6½" strips
- (24) 2½" squares

All blocks are made the same – but the color placement changes so we will **make 8** of Block A and **8** of Block B.

2 block a

Begin in the center and work toward the outer edge.

Sew a print 2½" square to either side of a background 2½" square. **2A**

Sew a 2½" x 6½" background strip to the top and bottom of the center strip. **2B**

Add a 2½" x 6½" print strip to either side of the center. **2C**

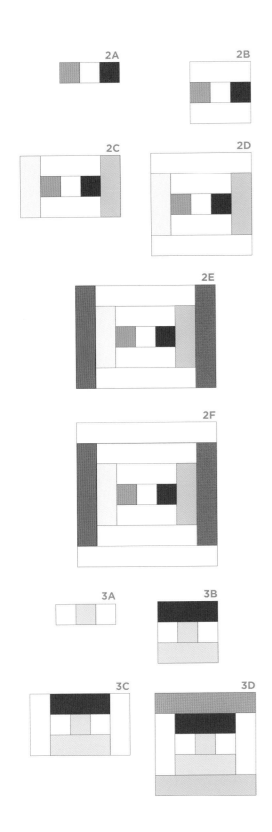

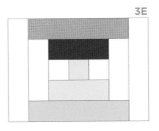

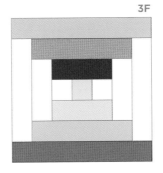

Sew a background 2½" square to either side of a print 2½" square. **3A**

Sew a print 2½" x 6½" strip to top and bottom of the center strip. **3B**

Add a 2½" x 6½" background strip to either side of the center. **3C**

Sew a 2½" x 10½" print strip to the top and bottom of the center. **3D**

Add a 2½" x 10½" background strip to either side of the center. **3E**

Sew a 2½" x 14½" print strip to the top and bottom of the center to complete the block. **Make 8. 3F**

Block Size: 14" Finished

Sew a 2½" x 10½" background strip to the top and bottom of the center. **2D**

Add a 2½" x 10½" print strip to either side of the center. **2E**

Sew a 2½" x 14½" background strip to the top and bottom of the center to complete the block.
Make 8. 2F

3 block b

Begin in the center and work toward the outer edge.

4 arrange and sew

Lay out the blocks in **rows of 4.** Begin row 1 and row 3 with Block B and alternate with Block A.

Begin rows 2 and 4 with Block A and alternate with Block B.

 NOTE: *Block A is rotated a quarter turn. When you are satisfied with the layout, sew the blocks together, then sew the rows together to complete the center of the quilt.*

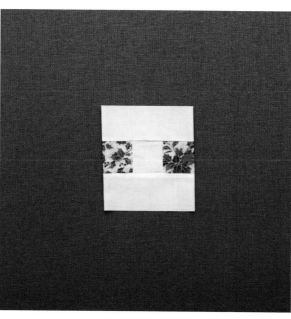

1 Sew a print 2½″ square to either side of a background 2½″ square.

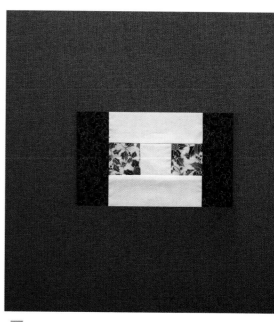

2 Add a background 2½″ x 6½″ strips to the top and bottom of the center strip.

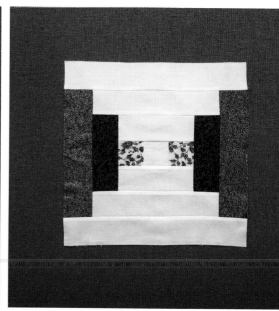

3 Add 2½″ x 6½″ print strip to both sides of the block.

4 Add a 2½″ x 10½″ background strip to the top and bottom.

5 Sew a print 2½″ x 10½″ strip to either side.

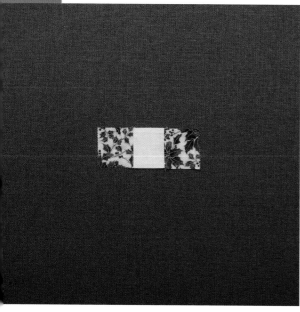

6 Add a 2½″ x 14½″ background strip to the top and bottom to complete a block A. The colors will be reversed when making block B.

5 first & third narrow borders

Cut (13) 1½" strips across the width of the fabric. Sew the strips together end-to-end to make one long strip. Trim the first and third narrow borders from this strip.

Refer to Borders (pg. 108) in the Construction Basics to measure and cut the inner borders. The strips are approximately 56½" for the sides and approximately 58½" for the top and bottom. For the third narrow border, the strips for the sides are approximately 63½" for the sides and approximately 65½" for the top and bottom.

6 second border-pieced

Cut the leftover strips into 3" increments for a **total of 122.** Make a 3" wide unfinished side border by sewing 29 pieces together. Make 2 and sew one to either side of the quilt. Sew 32 pieces together to make the 3" unfinished top border and repeat for the bottom border. Sew one to the top of the quilt and one to the bottom.

Refer to Borders (pg. 108) in the Construction Basics to measure and adjust the pieced borders if necessary. If you find the borders aren't quite working, use a smaller seam allowance or a larger one to compensate for the measurement being a little off. If you make the adjustments small and do it over several pieces, it won't be noticeable. The strips are approximately 58½" for the sides and approximately 63½" for the top and bottom.

7 outer border

Cut (8) 6" strips across the width of the fabric. Sew the strips together end-to-end to make one long strip. Trim the borders from this strip.

Refer to Borders, (pg. 108) in the Construction Basics to measure and cut the outer border. The strips are approximately 65½" for the sides and approximately 76½" for the top and bottom.

8 quilt and bind

Layer the quilt with batting and backing and quilt. After the quilting is complete, square up the quilt and trim away all excess batting and backing. Add binding to complete the quilt. See Construction Basics (pg. 109) for binding instructions.

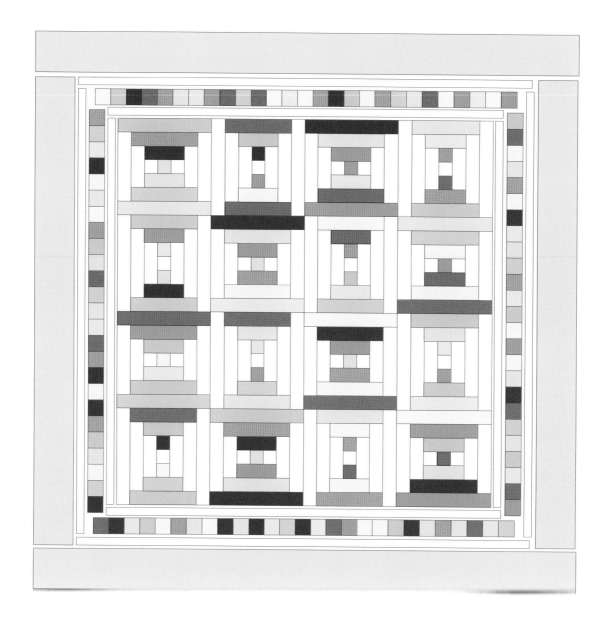

For the tutorial and everything
you need to make this quilt visit:
www.msqc.co/blockholiday16

cutting corners

quilt designed by *Missouri Star Quilt Company*

It takes a village to run a company like Missouri Star Quilt Co. From the very beginning, our dear friends and neighbors have been the wind beneath our wings and we are very grateful to them. The story of MSQC would never have continued without the support of family and friends.

In the early days, when we were in our first little brick building, the word hadn't really gotten out yet about our machine quilting services. We only had one machine and we couldn't keep it busy all day long like we do now! But every now and then I would get the opportunity to quilt beautiful heirloom quilts that our neighbors brought in out of the goodness of their hearts. Two darling sisters, Bernice and Deloris, had been taught by their mother to sew by hand. They would sit for hours and make huge quilts that they cut and sewed manually. Believe it or not, they never used a sewing machine! I had tried quilting by hand and knew it wasn't for me. So these sweet ladies would bring me their marvelous quilts to finish on my machine and I was amazed at how perfect and beautiful they were. They would finish at least one quilt a month—and I think they literally kept us in business that first year! We got to be good friends and they always supported us in everything we did.

To encourage visitors to come to the store, we started a little open sewing time called Friday Night Sew and, of course, Bernice and Deloris were right there. They also helped us start a Quilt Guild in Hamilton. There weren't many of us at the

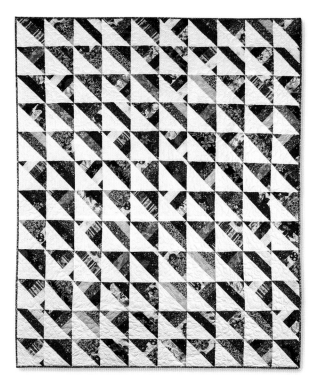

first few meetings, but we relished the time we spent together and built strong friendships that have lasted to this day.

The time came sooner than we expected to expand our main store and those dear ladies showed up to help with their husbands, Bob and James. They asked if there was anything they could do to help, and we emphatically said that there was. Those poor folks had no idea what they were in for! We were going from just a few shelves to 80 and we weren't sure how we were going to make them all! Thankfully, Bob and James had some experience and they showed up the very next day, tools in hand, all geared up to build shelves. These kind men had both been retired for some time and at one point I remember James saying that he didn't even know he could work like that anymore, and yet they still kept showing up to help.

One year around Christmastime, Bernice and Deloris noticed how tired I looked and asked again if they could help me by doing some of the binding on the quilts that were coming in. I told them they would have to pass a "binding test", which made them smile. When they showed me their stitches, I told them if they could just make them a little bigger and sloppier, they would look just like mine! They giggled. These girls have done all the binding on all my quilts ever since and I am so grateful for their love and support!

A few years have passed now and Bernice and Deloris are still binding away. When it came time for the Grand Re-opening in June, we told their husbands to put their hammers away and just bring themselves! Of course they showed up to support us and I felt like they were guests of honor after all they'd done to help Missouri Star get to where we are today.

materials

makes a 60" x 72" quilt

QUILT TOP
- 1 roll 2½" strips
- 2½ yards background

BINDING
- ¾ yard

BACKING
- 3¾ yards - horizontal seam(s)

SAMPLE QUILT
- **Holiday Flourish Silver** by Peggy Toole for Robert Kaufman

1 sew strip set

Sew (5) 2½" strips together. Cut each strip set into (4) 10" units. Trim each to 10" square. **Make 8 sets** for a **total of 32 squares.** Set 2 squares aside for another project. 1A

2 make blocks

From the background fabric, cut:

- (8) 10" strips across the width of the fabric - Subcut the strips into (30) 10" squares.

3A

3 make half-square triangles

Layer a 10″ background square with a 10″ square cut from the strip set with right sides facing. Sew all the way around the perimeter using a ¼″ seam allowance. 3A

Cut the sewn squares from corner to corner twice on the diagonal to make 4 half-square triangle units. Open each, press and square to 6½″. Repeat for the remaining 29 blocks for a **total of 120 half-square triangles.** 3B

Block Size: 6″ x 6″ Finished

3B

4 arrange in rows

Arrange the half-square triangles into **12 rows,** with each row having **10 blocks.** Sew the blocks together and press. Press the seam allowances of the odd numbered rows toward the right and the even numbered rows toward the left. Sew the rows together to complete the top.

5 quilt and bind

Layer the quilt with batting and backing and quilt. After the quilting is complete, square up the quilt and trim away all excess batting and backing. Add binding to complete the quilt. See Construction Basics (pg. 109) for binding instructions.

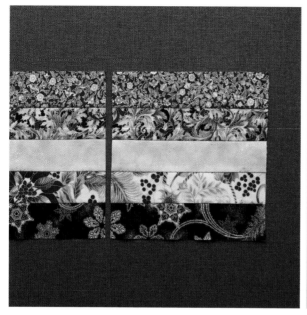

1 Sew (5) 2½" strips together. Cut the strip set into (4) 10" squares. Make sure your squares measure 10" on all sides.

2 Layer a 10" background square with a 10" strip set square. Sew all the way around the perimeter using a ¼" seam allowance.

3 Cut the sewn squares from corner to corner twice on the diagonal.

4 Open and press the seam allowance toward the darker fabric.

For the tutorial and everything you need to make this quilt visit:
www.msqc.co/blockholiday16

sashed
tumbler

quilt designed by *Missouri Star Quilt Company*

Whenever I hear a siren it reminds me of Christmas. No, it's not because I overbaked a batch of cookies once on Christmas Eve. It's because every year our Santa comes in on a big, red fire truck! In Hamilton, Missouri, the Christmas season begins one week before Thanksgiving with a town-wide lighting ceremony.

The main street is dressed to the nines in sparkling lights and tinsel. In preparation for the ceremony, City Hall sets up a whole forest of decorated trees in the park, and MSQC chips in by creating a handful of what are known as "magic trees"— non-pines that have been covered in literally hundreds of strings of lights. Lights are also strung all along our beautiful old buildings, and each bulb is tested to make sure it's ready for the big moment! All of this prep work is done with the greatest of care so that when the switch is flipped, everything goes off without a hitch!

The ceremony itself is a small but lively gathering. We have a canned food drive, an ugly sweater contest, and awards for the

69

best decorated shop window. This festive occasion brings friends and neighbors together to mingle and chat over steaming cups of hot chocolate. Finally, we gather close to the main stage and begin to sing carols. There may be a few stray notes here and there, but we sing together and we sing from the heart.

Then comes the big moment. A huge, decorative light switch is displayed on the stage, and as the crowd counts down from ten, someone, somewhere is secretly positioned with an extension cord, waiting to plug it in just as the switch is thrown.

photo credit: Caldwell County News

All at once a siren rings out from the distance. It gets louder and louder until finally, a fire truck carrying Mr. and Mrs. Claus comes rolling around the corner! The air is filled with excitement as the truck stops in the midst of the crowd. Santa helps Mrs. Claus down and they smile cheerfully as they greet each child with a hearty, "Ho! Ho! Ho!"

There is such a feeling of goodness and unity at our lighting ceremony; it's the perfect start to the most wonderful time of the year! If you're ever in town the week before Thanksgiving, we'd love to have you join us as we welcome our small town Santa on his fire truck.

" There may be a few stray notes here and there, but we sing together and we sing from the heart. "

materials

makes a 56" X 77" quilt

QUILT TOP
• 3 packages of 5″ squares

SASHING
• 2 yards

BORDER
• 1¼ yards

BINDING
• ¾ yard

BACKING
• 4¾ yards - vertical seam(s)

ADDITIONAL SUPPLIES
• MSQC 5″ Tumbler Template

SAMPLE QUILT
• **Just Be Claus** by Maywood Studio

1 cut

From the 3 packages of 5″ print squares, cut **120 tumblers** using the MSQC Tumbler Template. You can cut several tumblers at once by stacking 4-6 squares together and cutting around the template using your rotary cutter.

From the background fabric cut:

• (2) 5″ strips across the width of the fabric = subcut the strips into 5″ squares. You need a total of **12 squares.** Use the MSQC Tumbler Template to cut 12 tumbler shapes. Cut each tumbler shape in half vertically. **1A**

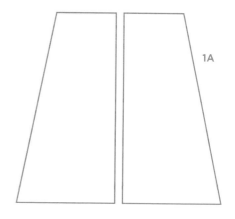

1A

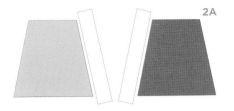

2A

- (35) 1½" strips across the width of the fabric. Subcut 18 strips into 5¾" increments for a total of (120) 1½" x 5¾" rectangles. Set the rest of the strips aside for the moment.

2 sew

Sew a 1½" x 5¾" sashing rectangle to the right-hand side of 60 tumblers and to the left-hand side of 48 tumblers. There will be no sashing on 12 tumblers.

2B

Trim the top and bottom of the sashing rectangle even with the top and bottom of the tumblers. **Make 108.** 2B

3 arrange and sew

Arrange the sashed tumblers into **12 rows** with each row having **10 tumblers.** Alternate the tumblers that have the sashing on the right with those that have the sashing on the left. Complete the row with a tumbler with no sashing. Notice that every other tumbler is turned 180-degrees. Make sure every row begins and ends with a tumbler that has no sashing on the outer edge. 3A

3A

Once you are happy with the arrangement, sew the tumblers into rows and add a half tumbler to both ends of each row. 3B

3B

4 make long sashing strips

Measure the rows. Each should measure approximately 47" wide. Make **13 long sashing strips** to match your measurement.

Sew the rows together, adding a long sashing strip between each row as well as one to the top and one to the bottom of the quilt.

5 borders

From the outer border fabric, cut:

- (7) 5½" strips across the width of the fabric. Sew the strips together end-to-end to make one long strip. Trim the borders from this strip.

Refer to Borders (pg. 108) in the Construction Basics to measure and cut the outer borders. The strips are approximately 67½" for the sides and approximately 56½" for the top and bottom.

6 quilt and bind

Layer the quilt with batting and backing and quilt. After the quilting is complete, square up the quilt and trim away all excess batting and backing. Add binding to complete the quilt. See Construction Basics (pg. 109) for binding instructions.

1 Using the 5″ Tumbler Template, cut 120 shapes from the 5″ print squares.

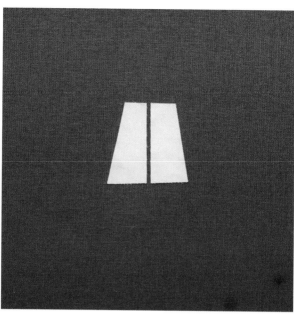

2 Cut 12 tumblers from the background fabric. Cut the tumblers in half vertically. Use the pieces at the end of each row.

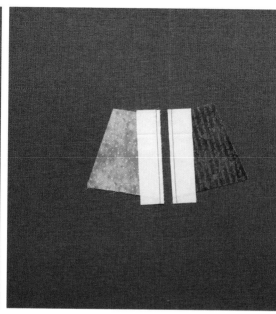

3 Sew a sashing strip to right-hand side of 60 tumblers and to the left-hand side of 48 tumblers.

4 Open and press the seam allowances toward the darker fabric.

5 Sew the tumblers together into rows.

For the tutorial and everything you need to make this quilt visit:
www.msqc.co/blockholiday16

4-patch

lattice

quilt designed by *Missouri Star Quilt Company*

Autumn just might be my favorite time of the year. Shh ... don't tell summer! Thinking of the changing leaves, crisp air, ripe fruits and vegetables, and harvest celebrations make me want to throw on a scarf and bake a pumpkin pie right now! When the kids were growing up, they also loved fall, but for a different reason. They eagerly anticipated the coming of Halloween with multiple costume changes and enthusiastic shouts of "trick-or-treat!", with all its variations, as they practiced for the big day.

As you know, we live in a small town and trick-or-treating was done before we knew it, so we liked to have a little celebration of our own before the kids went out that night. Each year we thought of different activities the kids and their friends might like and we've had backyard carnivals, homemade haunted houses, and other fun activities, but one year in particular, the kids had this idea that they wanted to have a mystery dinner with their friends.

So what's a mystery dinner, you might ask? The kids drew up a menu with grisly items like eyeballs, intestines, witch fingers, dragon's blood, and so on. Each item had a corresponding real-life entree and the goal was to get the right things together. You wanted to pick the intestines to go with the dragon's blood so that your spaghetti had sauce to go with it, but not every child figured that out! It was a hoot to watch those kids struggling to order the right menu items. One poor little guy ended up with spaghetti sauce, a cookie, and some peeled grapes, but he was a good sport. They all loved dressing up in their costumes and sitting at a big table together, eating their oddly assorted dinners. And honestly, I didn't mind all the cooking I had to do to make that night special for them. Although, we were eating spaghetti for a couple nights after that!

Afterwards, with full tummies and spaghetti-stained faces, the kids went out trick-or-treating and came home with large pillowcases filled with candy. Even though our neighbors are few, they are very generous! I'll always have fond memories of Halloween with my spirited, creative children and I love that I still get to host the grandchildren before they go out trick-or-treating. The rule is they have to eat a little dinner before they get candy, but who wants spaghetti when there's fun size candy bars calling your name?!

They eagerly anticipated the coming of Halloween with multiple costume changes and enthusiastic shouts of "trick-or-treat!", with all its variations, as they practiced for the big day.

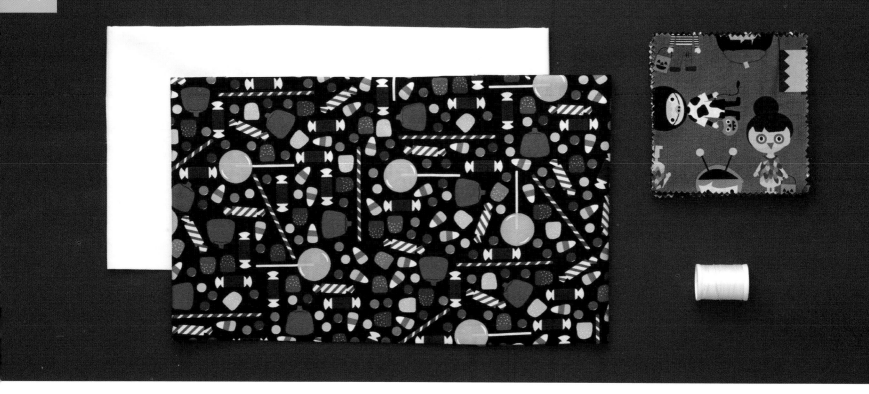

materials

makes a 67" X 76" quilt

QUILT TOP
- 4 packages of 5" squares (42 ct.)
- 1 yard contrasting fabric for lattice strips – includes inner border

BORDER
- 1¼ yards

BINDING
- ¾ yard

BACKING
- 4¾ yards - vertical seam(s)

SAMPLE QUILT
- **Pumpkin Fun** by Ann Kelle for Robert Kaufman

1 cut

From the contrasting fabric, cut:

- (14) 1½" strips across the width of the fabric. Subcut each strip into (3) 14" lengths for a total of (42) 1½" x 14" rectangles. Set the remaining fabric aside for the inner border.

2 make blocks

Make a 4-patch block by sewing (4) 5" squares together. Begin by sewing 2 squares together into a pair. **Make 2 pair.** Press the seam allowances in opposite directions then sew the 2 pairs together. **2A**

2A

2B

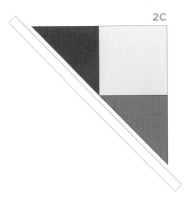

Slice the 4-patch block from corner to corner once on the diagonal. **2B**

Fold a 1½" x 14" rectangle in half. Mark the fold by finger-pressing a crease in place. Align the crease in the rectangle with the center point of the sliced 4-patch and pin. Pin in several places along the length of the strip. Stitch the rectangle to the sliced 4-patch using a ¼" seam allowance. **2C**

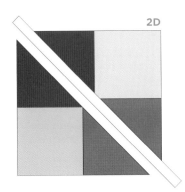

Repeat for the opposite side of the sliced 4-patch. **2D**

Make 42 blocks and trim each to 9½" square. **2E**

Block Size: 9" x 9" Finished

3 lay out blocks

Arrange the blocks in rows. Each row is made using **6 blocks** and you need to make **7 rows.** Rotate the blocks so the center strips weave through the quilt as shown in diagram **2F**. Press the seam allowances of the even numbered rows toward the left and the odd numbered rows toward the right so the blocks will nest.

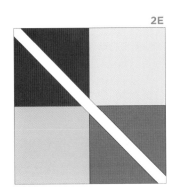

Sew the rows together to complete the center of the top.

4 inner border

Cut (7) 1½" strips across the width of the fabric. Sew the strips together end-to-end to make one long strip. Trim the borders from this strip.

Refer to Borders (pg. 108) in the Construction Basics to measure and cut the inner borders. The strips are approximately 63½" for the sides and approximately 56½" for the top and bottom.

5 outer border

Cut (7) 6" strips across the width of the fabric. Sew the strips together end-to-end to make one long strip. Trim the borders from this strip.

Refer to Borders (pg. 108) in the Construction Basics to measure and cut the outer borders. The strips are approximately 65½" for the sides and approximately 67½" for the top and bottom.

6 quilt and bind

Layer the quilt with batting and backing and quilt. After the quilting is complete, square up the quilt and trim away all excess batting and backing. Add binding to complete the quilt. See Construction Basics (pg. 109) for binding instructions.

1 Sew 5″ squares together into pairs. Make (2) per block.

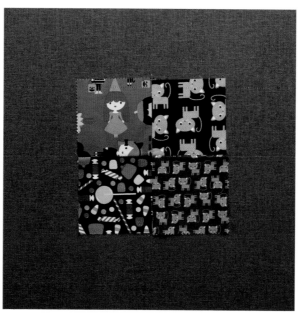

2 Sew (2) pairs together to make a 4-patch.

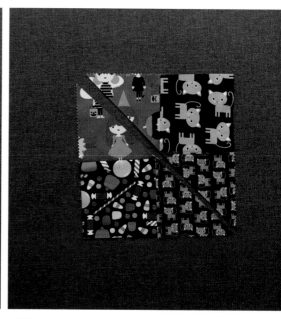

3 Cut each 4-patch from corner to corner once on the diagonal

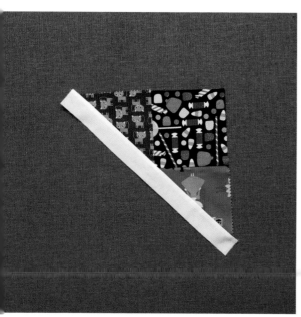

4 Sew a 1½″ x 14″ rectangle to one side of the sliced 4-patch.

5 Stitch the remaining side of the 4-patch to the other side of the rectangle.

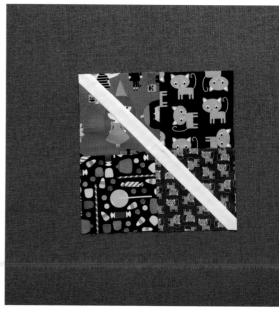

6 Press the seam allowances toward the darker fabric after the block is completed.

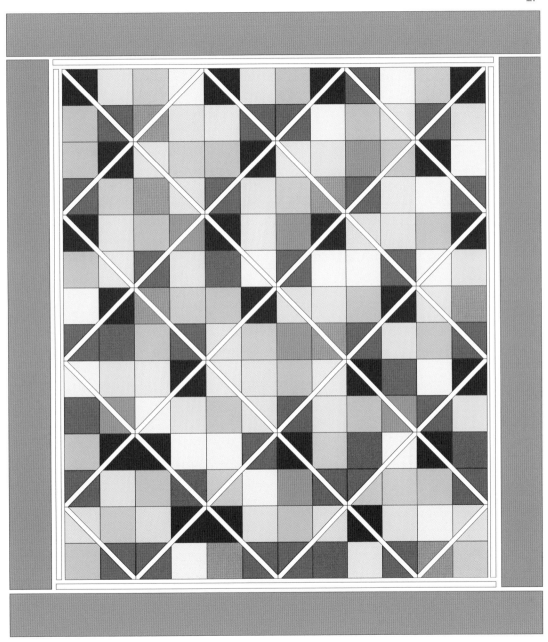

For the tutorial and everything you need to make this quilt visit:
www.msqc.co/blockholiday16

starburst

quilt designed by *Missouri Star Quilt Company*

I love Halloween and I dress up whenever I get the chance. After working as a costumer for years, I like to get really creative and ambitious with my costume ideas. And as a mother of seven, I've learned to make do with what I have rather than spend a lot of money on brand new supplies. Even the neighbor's kids would come to me for help! One year, after searching high and low for just the right costume, one of Al's friends told me he was cooking up a unique costume from the local church's old Christmas decorations. He was a teenager and was tired of just any old costume idea; he really wanted it to be spectacular. I couldn't wait to see what he had come up with.

Do you remember the little gold star stickers that, back in the day, teachers used in school? I don't know if that's still common, but in my day a gold star on a test or essay was high praise. I guess that's why I started saying "Gold star for you!" to the kids and their friends when they did something great. As they got older it became sort of a joke, which probably explains why that neighbor boy showed up to our Halloween party dressed as a gold star!

I'll admit it was hilarious, seeing this larger-than-life gold star waddle down the road, and we all agreed that he did, indeed, deserve a gold star for creativity. But when we headed inside for donuts he realized, for the first time, that his brilliant plan had overlooked one important fact: a refurbished outdoor Nativity star doesn't fit through your average doorway! And when he finally unhooked, unhinged, and unbuttoned everything he needed to in order to get the thing off, we decided that "Guy-In-His-Skivvies" might not be as creative a costume as a large gold star, but it was at least as funny!

"After working as a costumer for years, I like to get really creative and ambitious with my costume ideas."

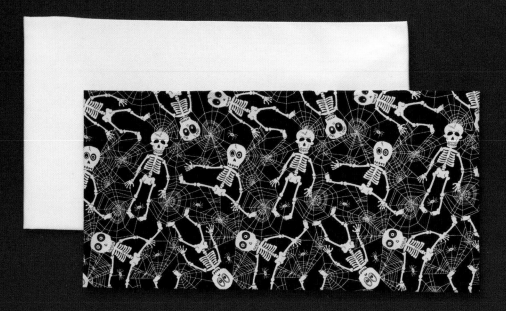 

materials

makes a 58" X 58" quilt

QUILT TOP
- 1 package 10″ print squares
- 1¼ yards background

BORDER
- 1 yard

BINDING
- ¾ yard

BACKING
- 3¾ yards - vertical seam(s)

SAMPLE QUILT
- **The Boo Crew** by Blank Studios

1 cut

From the background fabric, cut:

- (4) 10″ strips across the width of the fabric – subcut the strips into 10″ squares for a **total of 16.**

2 sew

Select (16) 10″ print squares from the package. Layer a background 10″ square with a print 10″ square with right sides facing. Sew all the way around the perimeter using a ¼″ seam allowance. **2A** Cut from corner to corner twice on the diagonal to make 4 half-square triangles.

2A

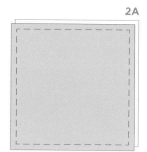
2B

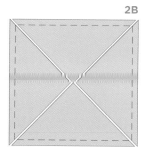

2C

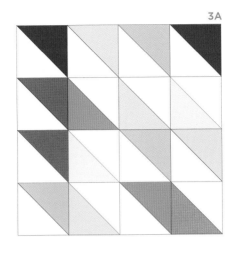
3A

Open and press the seam allowances toward the darkest fabric. 2B

Make 64 half-square triangles. 2C

3 lay out and sew

Lay out the half-square triangles in rows of **4 across** and **4 down.** Sew the rows together. This will make one quadrant of the quilt. **Make 4.** 3A

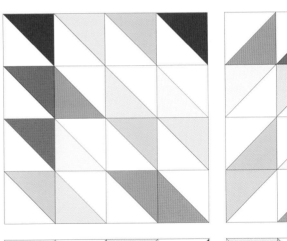

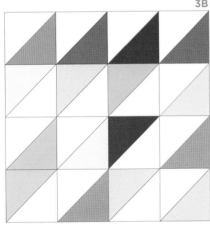
3B

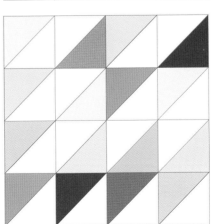

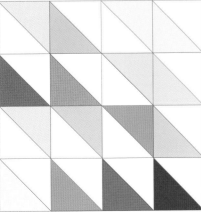

Once you have the 4 quadrants made, lay them out as shown and sew them together. 3B

4 border

Cut (6) 4½" strips across the width of the fabric. Sew the strips together end-to-end to make one long strip. Trim the borders from this strip.

Refer to Borders (pg. 108) in the Construction Basics to measure and cut the outer borders. The strips are approximately 50½" for the sides and approximately 58½" for the top and bottom.

5 quilt and bind

Layer the quilt with batting and backing and quilt. After the quilting is complete, square up the quilt and trim away all excess batting and backing. Add binding to complete the quilt. See Construction Basics (pg. 109) for binding instructions.

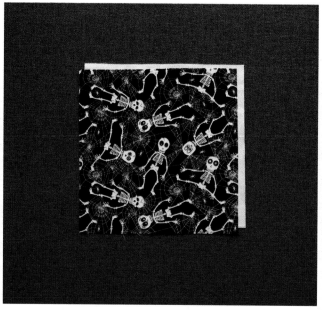

1 Layer a print 10″ square with a background 10″ square.

2 Sew all the way around the perimeter using a ¼″ seam allowance.

3 Cut the sewn square from corner to corner twice on the diagonal.

4 Open the half-square triangles and press the seam allowances toward the darker fabric. Follow the diagram on page 87 to make the quadrants for the quilt.

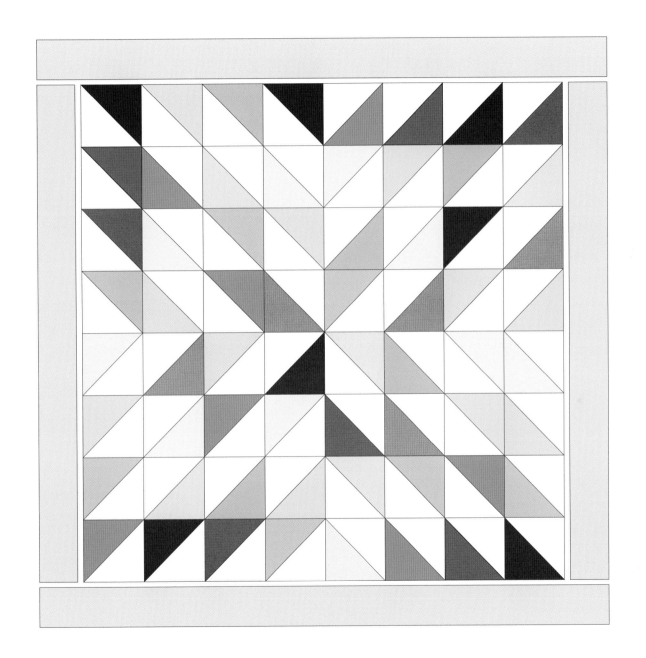

festive
rope bowls

We love making sweet gifts for our friends and family. Stitch up quick and easy rope baskets and fill them with gifts or use them to organize your home. They're so much fun to make, you'll want to give them to all your friends!

These charming baskets can be filled with treats like homemade cookies or candy and make the perfect gift for children and grown-ups alike. A basket filled with Legos would delight any child. Use them to hold hair bows, barrettes, or doll accessories. Precious rocks or little cars can find a home in a basket, tucked away safely. No matter how you use them, these versatile rope baskets can be personalized to add color and charm to your home.

Get Ready!
Gather up these supplies before you begin.

- Cotton Clothesline Rope
- Straight Pins
- Glue Stick – We like using Lapel Stick!
- 2½″ Fabric Strips
- Thread – Colors that contrast with your fabric strips add a little pizzazz!

Get Set!
Cut off a piece of clothesline rope that measures about 75″ in length.

Dab a bit of glue to the end of a fabric strip.

Glue the fabric strip to one end of the rope. Start wrapping the strip around the clothesline. Make sure you're wrapping the strip at an angle and keep it as tight as possible. Each strip should overlap the previous one with no rope showing.

When you reach the end of the strip of fabric, glue another strip onto the first and continue wrapping. You can mix or match your strips if you would like a multi-colored bowl.

Continue wrapping and adding strips until you literally reach the end of your rope. Glue the end of your fabric strip to the clothesline and give it a few minutes to dry.

After the glue is dry and the strip is securely in place, coil the end of the wrapped rope to form a circle, which will be the base of your basket. The coil should be about 5 rounds across.

Once you have completed the coil, stick a pin through the outer edge toward the center. Do that at four different places to keep it from unwinding.

Sew!
To make the base of the basket, sew straight across the coil between the pins using a straight stitch. Begin and end the seam with a few backstitches. Sew two more seams across the coil, making an X and removing the pins as you sew. Don't forget to backstitch at the beginning and the end of your seams.

Now it's time to build the sides of the basket. Set your sewing machine stitch to a wide zigzag. You'll need to make sure the needle crosses over and catches both sides of the coil as you sew.

Hold the base of the basket at a slight angle so it's tipped slightly on its side.

Begin sewing the loose cord to the base, keeping the angle steady and being careful to keep each round touching as you sew.

Continue sewing while keeping the basket at an angle. The depth of your basket depends on the angle you use while sewing. A soft angle will result in a wider, shallower basket. A sharper angle will make a basket that is deeper and narrower across.

When you reach the end of the wrapped cord, simply backstitch to secure the end in place. You did it! Look at that charming little basket you just made!

You don't have to stop there. Try making baskets any size you please simply by changing the length of the clothesline. We bet you can't make just one!

1 **Wrap a length of clothesline rope with fabric strips**

2 **Coil the end of the rope around about 5 times to make a small base. When you are happy with the base, stick a pin through the outside of the coil toward the center. Repeat and add 3 more pins.**

3 **Sew across the center of the coil, beginning and ending with a backstitch. Sew two more seams, making an X.**

4 **Set your sewing machine stitch to a wide zigzag and hold the bowl at a slight angle as you sew the rope to the base.**

5   **When you reach the end of the cord, simply backstitch to secure the end in place.**

Fabriflair™ dimensional star

Vintage made modern is my mantra! Amongst my collection of rare fabrics, antique quilts, and embroidered heirlooms is a unique 1930's dimensional star that inspired my new Indygo Junction product line, Fabriflair.

So what exactly is Fabriflair? Think of them as material amusements for needle and thread. To make these intriguing three dimensional shapes, all you have to do is cover precut matboard templates with your favorite fabrics and hand stitch them together into functional and decorative objects.

I love to customize Fabriflair for gift giving. Maybe you've got a sports fan in the family who'd love a personalized Brio Sphere featuring

their favorite team's fabric or you'd like to welcome in the newest baby with an embroidered Baby's First Christmas ornament. These meaningful keepsakes can be easily created with our kits.

Now that you know what Fabriflair is about, I've got a few tips and tricks that will make your experience even better. First off, you'll want to cut your fabric pieces with at least a ⅜" seam allowance so that they can easily wrap around the matboard pieces. Once you've done that step, secure the fabric on the back of the pieces with a little glue. It's important to use a fabric glue stick and be sure the glue dries before you stitch the pieces together. Fabric slipping and sliding makes it difficult to stitch pieces together, so be patient with this step. Next, you'll want to stitch all the pieces together. Make sure you sew through the fabric only on the edge of the template, not the matboard. I like to use a simple whipstitch. To make a Radiant Star, join 5 fabric-covered

diamond pieces together to make a star shape and repeat this step 12 times. Then stitch the 12 star shapes into the dimensional radiant star. Voila! You did it! Now you've got to try all the other awesome shapes.

Visit our website to browse a variety of Fabriflair kits, which include precut matboard template pieces and complete instructions, just add your favorite fabrics! Precuts are perfect for Fabriflair as they have coordinated prints all ready to assemble. You can choose from nifty little tri-fold needle books, pyramid shaped Trilliant ornaments, Brio Spheres with pentagonal pieces, and Radiant Stars, which are made up with a myriad of diamond shapes. Each is so much fun to make. They're pleasing puzzles made of beautiful fabrics. We offer the Radiant Star you see pictured as a kit in a 5" or 10" version. Try Fabriflair today and make something unique!

Amy Barickman, founder of Indygo Junction and Amy Barickman.com has published nearly 1200 patterns and 80 books during her tenure in the fabric arts industry. Titles include Amy Barickman's Vintage Notions, Indygo Junction's Fabric Flowers, Dimensional Denim, and The Magic Pattern Book. Through her blogs, websites and e-newsletters, Amy inspires countless crafters to explore their own creative spirit and experiment with the newest sewing, fabric and crafting techniques. Keep up with Amy as she shares her ideas and inspiration at:

www.AmyBarickman.com
www.IndygoJunction.com

christmas tree skirt

TREE SKIRT SIZE
45" X 45"

DESIGNED/PIECED/QUILTED BY
Missouri Star Quilt Company

TREE SKIRT TOP
2 packages of 5" print squares

BORDER
¾ yard

BINDING AND TIES
¾ yard

BACKING
3 yards - vertical seam(s)

Optional - freezer paper

SAMPLE QUILT
Pixie Noel by Tasha Noel for
Riley Blake

ONLINE TUTORIALS
msqc.co/blockholiday16

QUILTING
Holly

PATTERN
pg. 34

courthouse steps

QUILT SIZE
76" X 76"

DESIGNED/PIECED/QUILTED BY
Missouri Star Quilt Company

QUILT TOP
1 roll of 2½" print strips
1 roll of 2½" background strips

NARROW INNER BORDERS
¾ yard background

outer border
1½" yards

BINDING
¾ yard

BACKING
4¾ yards - vertical seam(s)

SAMPLE QUILT
Holly Night Metallic by Sentimental Studios for Moda

ONLINE TUTORIALS
msqc.co/blockholiday16

QUILTING
Christmas Paisley

PATTERN
pg. 50

cutting
corners

QUILT SIZE
60" X 72"

DESIGNED/PIECED/QUILTED BY
Missouri Star Quilt Company

QUILT TOP
1 roll 2½" strips
2½ yards background

BINDING
¾ yard

BACKING
3¾ yards - horizontal seam(s)

SAMPLE QUILT
Holiday Flourish Silver by Peggy Toole
for Robert Kaufman

ONLINE TUTORIALS
msqc.co/blockholiday16

QUILTING
Meandering Snowflake

PATTERN
pg. 60

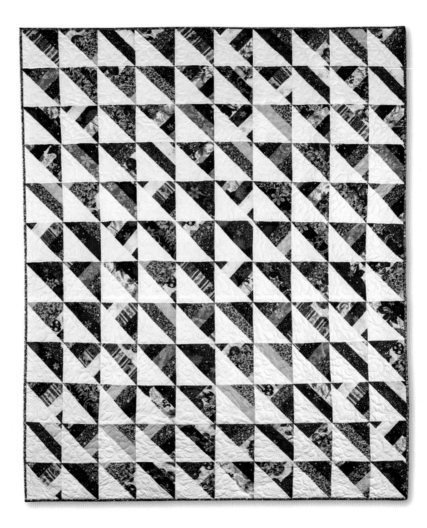

dashing stars

QUILT SIZE
90" X 90"

DESIGNED/PIECED/QUILTED BY
Missouri Star Quilt Company

QUILT TOP
1 package of 10" squares (42 ct.)
plus (3) 10" squares cut from outer
border fabric
3 yards background fabric – includes
sashing

INNER BORDER
¾ yard

OUTER BORDER
2 yards – includes fabric for cutting
(3) 10" squares for blocks and (4)
2½" squares for cornerstones

BINDING
¾ yard

BACKING
8¼ yards - vertical seams

SAMPLE QUILT
Scandi 3 by The Henley Studio for
Makower

ONLINE TUTORIALS
msqc.co/blockholiday16

QUILTING
Meandering Snowflake

PATTERN
pg. 16

dresden
wreath

QUILT SIZE
28" X 28"

DESIGNED/PIECED/QUILTED BY
Missouri Star Quilt Company

QUILT TOP
1 package 5" squares
¾ yard background fabric

BORDER
½ yard

BINDING
½ yard

BACKING
1 yard

ADDITIONAL SUPPLIES
MSQC Dresden Template

SAMPLE QUILT
Festive Fun by Lynette Anderson
Designs for RJR

ONLINE TUTORIALS
msqc.co/blockholiday16

QUILTING
Holly

PATTERN
pg. 26

4-patch lattice

QUILT SIZE
67" X 76"

DESIGNED/PIECED/QUILTED BY
Missouri Star Quilt Company

QUILT TOP
4 packages of 5" squares (42 ct.)
1 yard contrasting fabric for lattice
   strips – includes inner border

BORDER
1¼ yards

BINDING
¾ yard

BACKING
4¾ yards - vertical seam(s)

SAMPLE QUILT
Pumpkin Fun by Ann Kelle
for Robert Kaufman

ONLINE TUTORIALS
msqc.co/blockholiday16

QUILTING
Pumpkins

QUILT PATTERN
pg. 76

half-hexy snowman

QUILT SIZE
19¼" X 45"

DESIGNED/PIECED/QUILTED BY
Missouri Star Quilt Company

TABLE RUNNER TOP
(4) 10" white solid squares
(4) 10" assorted dark print squares
(2) 5" matching light print squares
(1) 10" dark solid square for buttons,
    mouths and eyes
(1) 2" x 4" scrap of orange for noses

SASHING, OUTER BORDER, BINDING
¾ yard dark print

OTHER SUPPLIES
10" x 12" rectangle paper-backed
    fusible web
MSQC 10" Half-Hexagon Template

BACKING
1½ yards

SAMPLE QUILT
Artisan Batiks Noel by Lunn Studios
for Robert Kaufman

ONLINE TUTORIALS
msqc.co/blockholiday16

QUILTING
Mitten Meander

QUILT PATTERN
pg. 8

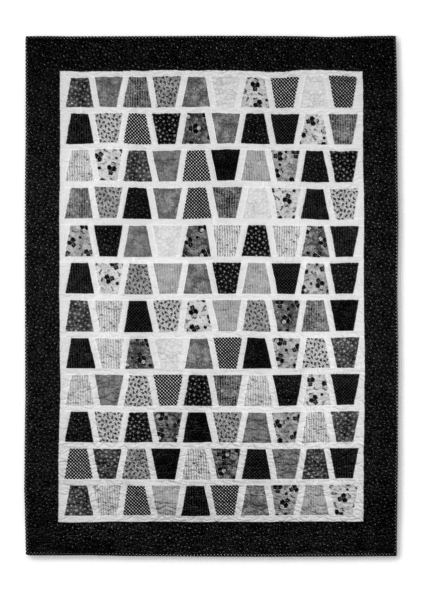

sashed tumbler

QUILT SIZE
56" X 77"

DESIGNED/PIECED/QUILTED BY
Missouri Star Quilt Company

QUILT TOP
3 packages of 5" squares

SASHING
2 yards

BORDER
1¼ yards

BINDING
¾ yard

BACKING
4¾ yards - vertical seam(s)

ADDITIONAL SUPPLIES
MSQC 5" Tumbler Template

SAMPLE QUILT
Just Be Claus by Maywood Studio

ONLINE TUTORIALS
msqc.co/blockholiday16

QUILTING
Meandering Snowflake

PATTERN
pg. 68

starburst

QUILT SIZE
58″ X 58″

DESIGNED/PIECED/QUILTED BY
Missouri Star Quilt Company

QUILT TOP
1 package 10″ print squares
1¼ yards background

BORDER
1 yard

BINDING
¾ yard

BACKING
3¾ yards - vertical seam(s)

SAMPLE QUILT
The Boo Crew by Blank Studios

ONLINE TUTORIALS
msqc.co/blockholiday16

QUILTING
Spiderwebs

PATTERN
pg. 84

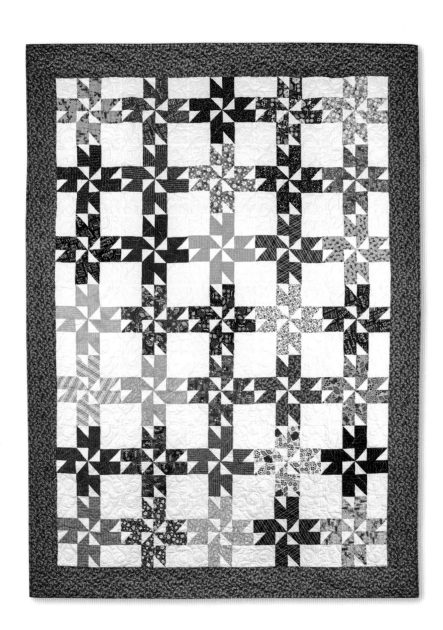

surprise pinwheel

QUILT SIZE
65" X 87"

DESIGNED/PIECED/QUILTED BY
Missouri Star Quilt Company

QUILT TOP
1 roll 2½" strips
3 yards background fabric

BORDER
1¼ yards

BINDING
¾ yard

BACKING
5¼ yards - vertical seam(s)

SAMPLE QUILT
Juniper Berry by BasicGrey for Moda

ONLINE TUTORIALS
msqc.co/blockholiday16

QUILTING
Holly

PATTERN
pg. 42

construction basics

- All seams are ¼" inch unless directions specify differently.

- Cutting instructions are given at the point when cutting is required.

- Precuts are not prewashed; therefore do not prewash other fabrics in the project

- All strips are cut WOF

- Remove all selvages

- All yardages based on 42" WOF

ACRONYMS USED

MSQC	Missouri Star Quilt Co.
RST	right sides together
WST	wrong sides together
HST	half-square triangle
WOF	width of fabric
LOF	length of fabric

pre-cut glossary

5" SQUARE PACK
1 = (42) 5" squares or ¾ yd of fabric
1 = baby
2 = crib
3 = lap
4 = twin

2½" STRIP ROLL
1 = (40) 2½" strip roll cut the width of fabric
      or 2¾ yds of fabric
1 = a twin
2 = queen

10" SQUARE PACK
1 = (42) 10" square pack of fabric: 2¾ yds total
1 = a twin
2 = queen

When we mention a precut, we are basing the pattern on a 40-42 count pack. Not all precuts have the same count, so be sure to check the count on your precut to make sure you have enough pieces to complete your project.

general quilting
- All seams are ¼" inch unless directions specify differently.
- Cutting instructions are given at the point when cutting is required.
- Precuts are not prewashed; therefore do not prewash other fabrics in the project.
- All strips are cut width of fabric.
- Remove all selvages.
- All yardages based on 42" width of fabric (WOF).

press seams
- Use the cotton setting on your iron when pressing.
- Press the seam just as it was sewn RST. This "sets" the seam.
- To set the seam, press just as it was sewn with right sides together.
- With dark fabric on top, lift the dark fabric and press back.
- The seam allowance is pressed toward the dark side. Some patterns may direct otherwise for certain situations.
- Press toward borders. Pieced borders may demand otherwise.
- Press diagonal seams open on binding to reduce bulk.

borders
- Always measure the quilt top 3 times before cutting borders.
- Start measuring about 4" in from each side and through the center vertically.
- Take the average of those 3 measurements.
- Cut 2 border strips to that size. Piece strips together if needed.
- Attach one to either side of the quilt.
- Position the border fabric on top as you sew. The feed dogs can act like rufflers. Having the border on top will prevent waviness and keep the quilt straight.
- Repeat this process for the top and bottom borders, measuring the width 3 times. Include the newly attached side borders in your measurements.
- Press toward the borders.

binding

find a video tutorial at: www.msqc.co/006

- Use 2½" strips for binding.
- Sew strips end-to-end into one long strip with diagonal seams, aka plus sign method (next). Press seams open.
- Fold in half lengthwise wrong sides together and press.
- The entire length should equal the outside dimension of the quilt plus 15" - 20."

plus sign method

- Lay one strip across the other as if to make a plus sign right sides together.
- Sew from top inside to bottom outside corners crossing the intersections of fabric as you sew. Trim excess to ¼" seam allowance.
- Press seam open.

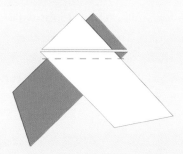

attach binding

- Match raw edges of folded binding to the quilt top edge.
- Leave a 10" tail at the beginning.
- Use a ¼" seam allowance.
- Start in the middle of a long straight side.

find a video tutorial at: www.msqc.co/001

10" tail   ¼"

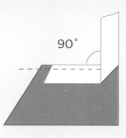

90°   fold

miter corners

- Stop sewing ¼" before the corner.
- Move the quilt out from under the presser foot.
- Clip the threads.
- Flip the binding up at a 90° angle to the edge just sewn.
- Fold the binding down along the next side to be sewn, aligning raw edges.
- The fold will lie along the edge just completed.
- Begin sewing on the fold.

close binding

*MSQC recommends **The Binding Tool** from TQM Products to finish binding perfectly every time.*

- Stop sewing when you have 12" left to reach the start.
- Where the binding tails come together, trim excess leaving only 2½" of overlap.
- It helps to pin or clip the quilt together at the two points where the binding starts and stops. This takes the pressure off of the binding tails while you work.
- Use the plus sign method to sew the two binding ends together, except this time when making the plus sign, match the edges. Using a pencil, mark your sewing line because you won't be able to see where the corners intersect. Sew across.

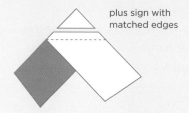

plus sign with matched edges

- Trim off excess; press seam open.
- Fold in half wrong sides together, and align all raw edges to the quilt top.
- Sew this last binding section to the quilt. Press.
- Turn the folded edge of the binding around to the back of the quilt and tack into place with an invisible stitch or machine stitch if you wish.

THE FAIR THIEF
PART 3
Red Herring
──── A JENNY DOAN MYSTERY ────
written by Steve Westover

Jenny paid the salesman and then accepted the surveillance drone from his chubby hands. It was even lighter than she had imagined. Turning to MK, Jenny grinned and said, "I have an idea."

MK watched the wheels spinning in Jenny's mind. She had seen this look on Jenny's face many times and MK knew it didn't always work out to her benefit. She bit the side of her lip as she cautiously asked, "Does this idea involve me going blind watching hours and hours and hours of surveillance tapes from last night?"

Jenny nodded and planted her fist with a slow-motion punch into MK's shoulder. "You've got it, champ."

MK groaned. Snatching the drone from Jenny she muttered something incomprehensible followed by, "hotel room."

"No, no. Don't take it back to the hotel," Jenny said.

"Watching the footage is only a small part of my plan." MK's head cocked as she waited to hear the rest. Jenny continued, "I want everyone to know you're watching the footage. In fact, I'm hoping Stephanie can help get that word out." Jenny looked around for a moment. "Where is Stephanie?"

"Well, you left her in your wake when you beelined it to the drone booth. I don't really know where ..." MK started to say. She chuckled with good humor, and a little jealousy, as Stephanie turned the corner, taking a bite of churro.

"Sorry. I got sidetracked," Stephanie said between bites.

"That's okay," Jenny said. "We have a plan but we could use your help."

Stephanie quickly finished chewing and became serious. "Of course. Anything."

MK's face twisted with displeasure as she retold Jenny's plan.

Jenny stretched her neck while she thought for a moment. Then she added, "Not only are we going to review the drone footage, but we need to do it in the most conspicuous manner possible. That's where you come in," Jenny said, turning towards Stephanie. "Can you casually spread the word around the vendors and amongst the fair officials that we have video evidence of the theft?"

Stephanie furrowed her brow. "Sure. I suppose. But what if the footage doesn't show anything? Shouldn't we wait until we know for sure?"

Jenny's sly grin grew into a full smile. "Oh, I doubt we'll find any useful evidence on the video. That angle and the distance aren't in our favor, but that's not exactly the point. I want to make the thief very nervous. We're just going to run a little con to force him ..."

"Or her," MK added.

"Right ... into the open. If he, or she, is worried about being discovered, maybe ..."

"Yeah, I got it," MK said. "I'm the bait to lure the thief."

"Technically, the drone recording is the bait," Stephanie corrected. "You'll just happen to be with that recording."

"Wow. I feel so much better," MK said.

"Don't worry. I think I see where Jenny's going with this. While you're reviewing the video for evidence, we'll have the drone hovering near your location to record any funny business," Stephanie said.

Jenny touched her forefinger to her nose. "Exactly. And MK, if you happen to take a little break, or three, leaving the video vulnerable, well then, we may just see who comes looking for it."

"What we need is the right location," Stephanie said. Jenny could feel the excitement building inside her. This might actually work! "The location needs to be accessible enough that the thief can get to it, but also isolated enough that someone's not going to innocently wander in. We need audio visual hookups for MK so she can watch the video and, ideally, a second set nearby for the DVR so we can record the new video from the drone."

"We can do this!" Stephanie grabbed the drone from MK and started rushing away. "Come on, MK. I know the perfect place to set up." Stephanie took two long steps and then stopped mid-stride. She turned back toward Jenny. "What are you going to do?"

Jenny's sly grin returned. "Not much, but there are a couple of people I want to talk to."
Stephanie's jaw set and she nodded sharply. "Let's do it."

***

Jenny had considered a few possibilities, but still hadn't decided upon a reasonable motive for the quilt thefts. Was someone merely planning to sell the stolen quilts? It sure felt like a lot of risk for a relatively small payout. Did the thief plan to steal the designs and sell them? Maybe publish the designs in a book or magazine? Again, the potential payout didn't seem to warrant the crime. Or maybe it wasn't about money at all. Maybe the motive had more to do with retaliation than greed.

Jenny immediately thought of the disqualified quilt from the handstitched contest the previous day. While the design had been expertly crafted and the quilt beautifully pieced, the use of a longarm stitcher had disqualified the quilt. Jenny could imagine the disappointment the quilter must have felt, and she knew quilters took their craft seriously. But still, it was hard to imagine a quilter betraying other quilters by stealing their work.

Jenny sighed with resignation as she began her slow walk back to the circus tent that doubled as the quilt gallery. Inside the tent, Jenny approached the disqualified quilt, happy it was still hanging in its place. She read the name on the tag out loud, "Judith Snelly. Hmm. Where are you,

Judith?" Knowing that it was unlikely the quilter would have let her work remain if she'd already left the fair, Jenny considered how she might find this woman. She could wait until Judith came to retrieve the quilt, but there was no telling how long that might take.

Near the back of the tent Martha sat with her eyes closed. The docent looked like she was recovering after a long day of tours even though it was still morning. When Jenny noticed her fellow judge, she approached quietly, but paused before speaking, not wanting to startle the woman. "Martha," she said gently and then waited. The woman didn't budge so Jenny called the name again, but louder, "Martha."

Martha slowly shifted in her seat and opened her eyes. She saw Jenny towering over her and her face flushed with embarrassment. "Hi, Jenny." Martha stood up carefully. "I thought you would have left by now. Are you feeling better?"

"Yes, Martha. I feel fine. Thank you. I'm hoping you can help me with something."

"Oh?"

"I'm investigating the quilt theft and I need a little information," Jenny said.

"I'll do what I can. It's such a shame about those quilts. Do you really think you can find them?" Martha asked.

"Well, we're doing our best. You met my assistant, MK. She's reviewing some video footage from last night to see if she can find anything suspicious, but I thought it might be wise to speak to Judith Snelly. She's the one who ..."

"Oh, yes. Of course, poor Judith. She was devastated when her quilt was disqualified."

"Do you know how to reach her? Do you have a cell phone number or something?" Jenny asked.
Martha thought for a moment. "No. I don't think so, but why don't we check the registration book. Maybe she listed it on her entry form." Martha walked slowly toward the front entrance of the tent. Behind a thin divider was small

red desk that had been distressed to make it look like an antique. Below the desk sat a plastic bin. Martha placed the bin on the desk and removed the lid. She fumbled through a notebook until she came to Judith's entry form. She removed it and handed it to Jenny. "I'm not sure how much this will help you."

Jenny read the paper. The shaky handwriting was difficult to read and the form was incomplete. It listed Judith's name and the name of her quilt, Seashore Village, but the personal information was mostly blank. No phone number. No email. And under the address portion was one word. Jenny held the paper close to her eyes as she concentrated on the illegible word. "Centralia? I think."

Jenny considered the name and then pulled out her phone. She typed in Judith Snelly, Centralia, Missouri, into her browser and clicked search. A link to a "person finder" website popped up, so she opened it. Within two clicks the site listed a full address and home phone number for Judith Snelly.

Jenny dialed the home phone number. After four rings an elderly gentleman answered, "Hello?"

Jenny cleared her throat softly and then spoke like personal friend, "Mr. Snelly, hi. This is Jenny. I'm down here at the fair and I'm trying to get a hold of Judith, but I misplaced her cell phone number. Can you help me?"

Mr. Snelly's tone brightened, "Sure. She's not home yet, but should be back in a couple of hours."

"Yes, I'd like to speak with her before she leaves the fair. Could you please give me her number?" Jenny prompted.

"I've got it here somewhere. I'm sure of it." Mr Snelly rustled through some papers. "Found it," He gave Jenny Judith's number. "And if you can't get a hold of Judith, try giving Tommy a call." He read off a second number and Jenny scribbled it down.

"Thank you very much, Mr. Snelly." Jenny hung up and examined her notes as Martha looked over her shoulder.

"Who's Tommy?" Martha asked.

Jenny had no idea, but it didn't matter because she had what she was looking for. She immediately dialed Judith's number and then invited the quilter to the gallery to talk. "Judith said she'll be here soon. She sounds really sweet."

"She is," Martha agreed. "You'll like her."

Jenny bit the inside of her lip. Judith was her best suspect. She hoped she wouldn't like her too much. Dialing again, Jenny spoke quickly once MK answered, "Are you ready to start viewing the video?"

"Stephanie's been jabbering to everyone we meet that we have evidence of the quilt theft. Most people don't have a clue what she's talking about. It's hilarious," MK said, but she didn't sound amused.

"That's great, but are you ready to watch the video?" Jenny repeated. MK became silent for a moment. She didn't speak, but Jenny could hear her breathing. "MK?"

"We hit a couple of snags, but we should be up and running in about ten minutes ... I think."

"What kind of snags?" Jenny asked.
MK laughed nervously. "Well, we realized we needed a little technical assistance."

"Assistance with what?" Jenny asked like a seasoned interrogator.

MK chuckled again, but her tone was anything but jovial.

"With everything, Jenny. We need help with everything. Okay. We couldn't figure out how to hook up the video to watch. We couldn't figure out how to get the drone to fly and hover and record and ... just everything. It's a mess."

Jenny treaded lightly. "So you found someone to help? That's great."

"Stephanie ran back to the drone shack to get their help. She'll be back soon. Gotta go. I'll keep you posted." MK hung up.

Jenny's eyebrows rose and she mumbled to herself as she recovered from MK's abrupt hang-up. "Wonderful. I love it when a plan comes together." Jenny flopped her head back so that she was staring at the ceiling of the tent and then said to Martha, "I may be in over my head."